MW01201984

LIGHTNING OVER THE TREASURY BUILDING

OR

*AN EXPOSE OF OUR BANKING AND CUR-
RENCY MONSTROSITY—AMERICA'S
MOST REPREHENSIBLE AND
UN-AMERICAN RACKET*

By

JOHN R. ELSOM

A CLEAR AND CONCISE TREATISE OF THE BANK-
ING AND MONEY SYSTEM OF THE UNITED STATES
AS MANIPULATED BY THE INTERNATIONAL
BANKERS, BY WHOM GOVERNMENTS ARE CON-
TROLLED, WARS PROMOTED, PEOPLES EXPLOITED
AND THE REAL WEALTH OF THE NATION GATH-
ERED UNTO THEMSELVES THROUGH THE PROCESS
OF MORTGAGE AND FORECLOSURE—TOGETHER
WITH A CONSTITUTIONAL REMEDY FOR OUR
NATIONAL DILEMMA.

SEVENTH PRINTING
Copyright 1941 by John R. Elsom

FORUM PUBLISHING COMPANY,
324 NEWBURY STREET,
BOSTON 15, MASSACHUSETTS

DEDICATION

To my desperately afflicted dear Old

UNCLE SAM

*Who, though possessing in his own splendid
Constitution, the means to make him well
and strong, stubbornly refuses to permit the
healing power to enter his emaciated system
and so is at the point of death, this little
Book is lovingly dedicated.*

JOHN R. ELSOM

ABRAHAM LINCOLN

After the passage of the National Banking
Act of 1863 and shortly before his
assassination, said:

"I see in the near future a crisis approaching that unnerves me and causes me to tremble for the safety of my
country; corporations have been enthroned, an era of corruption in High Places will follow, and the Money Power
of the Country will endeavor to prolong its reign by working upon the prejudices of the People, until the wealth is
aggregated in a few hands, and the Republic is destroyed."

HIS PROPHECY IS ALL BUT FULFILLED

TO ALL WHOM IT MAY CONCERN:

The Author hereby declares that he is an American, Loyal to the core to the American Flag, to the Republic of the United States of America, to its Constitution and form of Government; that he is of British descent, that his natural sentiments cause him to be strongly pro-British, and that the declarations of FACTS contained in this book are not a literary attack on England, nor any other nation or people within any other nation, but on a hybrid system of economy which, like a bloodsucking leech, attached itself in decades gone by, to the governments of the world, and which the Democracies must slough off, without delay, if they are to survive competition with the foreign Dictatorships which have already removed from their once emaciated bodies the disastrous, parasitical system of National Finance with which this book deals.

Loyalty to the Republic of the United States of America, demands this vigorous attack on the prevailing system of economy, which, because of long durance, is now generally considered as being an integral part of American policy, but which is as foreign to the truly American Way as a crowned Sovereign or ambitious Dictator would be.

After serious thought, and years of research, a loyal American writes, without rancor, for patriotic Americans who desire the truth but who, for lack of time or facilities, are frequently unable to make exhaustive study of matters which effect them the most.

CONTENTS

"Let me issue and control a nation's money and
I care not who writes its laws."
Amschel Rothschild.

INTRODUCTION

For several years the Author's blood has been kept at the boiling point by the legalized injustices of our inequitable, unethical, unworkable and unconstitutional debt and bond-based money system.

The knowledge that every dollar in circulation in America is a borrowed dollar and pays its toll of interest to the money-creating and money-manipulating Bankers—who contribute not a single thin dime of value in goods or productive services to the Nation's welfare—by which they skim off the cream, leaving but the pale blue milk for public use, was 'fuel in the furnace of his soul which threatened at times to blow his top off.

When it became necessary, under the present asinine system, to raise the Nation's debt ceiling to permit the *borrowing* of still other billions of dollars on interest bearing bonds, that the Nation might be placed irredeemably in hock to the Money Powers—while *Congress is authorized by the Constitution to do as Abraham Lincoln did in order to finance the Civil War*, to-wit: *issue the money required against the credit of the Nation, debt and interest free*— the internal pressure was so great that he all but exploded. Instead, the boiler pressure was relieved somewhat by the opening of the throttle in outspoken protest and definite action.

With his boiler pressure relieved somewhat by the running of the engine, he went to Washington to peer, if possible, behind the scenes to find out why our Treasury Department follows the ridiculous policy of printing money, giving it to the Bankers, then printing interest-bearing bonds, placing them in the vaults of the Bankers—*and then borrowing the money out and leaving the bonds in.*

He was determined to learn, if possible, how that process just described added anything to the soundness or value of the Nation's money and why the money required by the Government could not be printed by the Bureau of Printing and Engraving and used directly by Congress to pay the Nation's bills—without the formality of bonds and the requirement of interest to private Bankers.

As he sped over the rails to the seat of "Government of the People, by the People and for the People," his physical inactivity induced mental exertion. He tried to find, by logic, a reasonable answer to the riddle in advance of his arrival in Washington. But, although he might be able to disclose the mysteries of relativity; to explain with lucidity the fourth dimension; to divulge the secrets of atomic force, making clear the proportionate and relative position of the nucleus, the positron and the neutron, providing the driving force of the electron within the atom, within the molecule —of which all matter consists—but, *the question of why the Nation borrows its own money, based on its own credit, at interest, from private bankers, was too deep for him.*

The frustration caused by his inability to solve this apparently simple problem, caused his boiler pressure to rise once more, quite rapidly, to the exploding point.

Nature also took a hand. When he stepped from the air-conditioned coach in the Nation's Capital, where Democracy is on trial, he stepped into a veritable and sultry furnace. It was at the time of the "unusual" hot spell of the summer of 1940. The heat—internal and external— did its stuff.

It was five o'clock P.M., when he walked, eyes staring straight ahead, through the depot and out onto the sidewalk. There before him, at a little distance, stood the Capitol, but *it* held no interest for him. The *"Treasury Build-*

ing" was the one he wished to see. If it looked as crazy as our money system, he knew that he could spend a night of happy delirium just gazing at its ludicrous architecture.

Up to Pennsylvaia Avenue he strode, sweat oozing from every pore and lather forming around his collar, behind his ears and in his boots; jets of smoke and flame were emitted from ears and nostrils and sparks flew from his eyes as from an emery wheel.

He became the incarnation of the spirit of 160,000,000 informed Americans whose intelligence has been insulted. whose property has been confiscated, whose independence has been outraged—and indignation threatened momentarily to consume him as his brain was seared anew by thoughts that the Declaration of Independence and the Constitution of the United States have both been forgotten by the Government, and that the elected Representatives of the People have ignored their oaths of office, until the Nation has become the happy hunting ground of the special privileged few, who issue and control the Nation's purchasing power on a confiscatory basis.

As he made his way, furiously, toward the South, the evening sun blazed its fury on his right—while on his left the noble shaft of Washington's Monument pointed toward the throne of the Eternal God.

Unnoticed, from the South a messenger, borne on the wings of the wind, rode hard toward the North.

Crouching low beneath the ramparts of the jagged sky line, his rushing advance was as inexorable as the tide. His expansive breast was bursting with an awful, but righteous, wrath. In his mighty fist was unleashed fury.

The irate Author, arriving at Fifteenth Street, stopped dead in his tracks. There before him stood the *"Treasury Building."* He stood nonplussed, surveying its extensive proportions. Its sane architectural design belied the folly of its enterprise. It had been erected with skill and care, giving evidence that its builders were at least not quite mad.

He was confronted with the fact that his generation had retrogressed in understanding until now a structure designed and built by sane men of a former generation housed persons who were so mentally inert as to set themselves, and every person in the Nation toiling to pay interest on their own money, which, after having been created on their own credit, by their own endeavor, on their own machines, they gave to others—to borrow again that they might live, and wed and build and plow, and sow, and reap—and then lie down and die, having financed each detail with their own money given to and then borrowed at interest from other men.

At this thought he figuratively tore his hair, pawed the pavement, bellowed like an angry bull—jetted steam—and fire—and smoke. Would the accumulated force of the aggravated spirit of 160,000,000 informed Americans rend him asunder?

When the torrential billows of his rage had subsided, a grief as great as the interest burden carried by the staggering toilers of the Nation surged over his soul. All of the tragic despair of all who sought futilely for work; of all who had lost their homes to the interest gatherers; of all whose farms were foreclosed upon by the money lenders; of all who were suffering the pangs of hunger and who were forced to watch their loved ones wither and die in the midst of unlimited abundance, deluged him like a rushing flood.

"How long—Oh Lord—How Long?"—was the cry of his burdened heart.

Then appeared the August Messenger from the South. His features were awful to behold as he towered over *White House* and *Treasury Building*. He rolled in fury across the skies—dark and portending evil.

No sooner had the dark visaged messenger taken his position above the *Treasury Building*—his vast army strewn across the face of the sky behind him—than, with thunderous voice which shook the very foundations of the earth, he unsheathed a fiery sword with which he rent the heavens above the Building with a zigzag blow. It seemed that the Building must be split asunder and levelled with the pavement.

Again and again deep voiced bellows of outraged justice burst from the avenger's throat to roll across the face of the sky and cause the earth to tremble. And again and again the flaming sword, gripped firmly in the steely fist of Omnipotence, cleaved the sky with jagged blows.

But this display of indignation at the conniving deeds of unscrupulous and selfish men proved to be but a warning of impending doom if the intrigue to impoverish and enslave the sons of men were permitted to continue.

Soon the fury of the Righteous Messenger was spent. His warning message to the *White House, official Washington* and the *Treasury Department* had been faithfully delivered for *Him whose throne is established in truth and whose ways are past finding out.*

Instead of fire and brimstone, copious torrents of rain fell upon the sweltering city. The heat of atmosphere and body and mind was broken. The Author retired to his room, fatigued but content. His indignation was small compared with that of the Almighty. His power was puny compared with the strength of Jehovah. He, too, could wait—and waiting, labor for the establishment of truth, equity and righteousness on the earth, until the lion and the lamb could lie down together without the lamb being consumed by the lion.

"ALL OTHER REFORMS WAIT ON MONEY REFORM"
SO WHY WAIT TO REFORM MONEY?

Lightning Over the Treasury Building

CHAPTER I

THE GOLDSMITHS

Once upon a time, gold—being the most useless of all metals—was held in low esteem. Things which possessed intrinsic value were labored for—fought for—accumulated —and prized. These things became the standards of value and the mediums of exchange in the respective localities producing them.

One of the most urgent requirements of man is a wife, and it used to be that one of the most prized possessions of a father was a strong, hard working daughter; and she was considered his property. In those days he didn't give a dowry with her to get rid of her—but if a young blade desired her he had to recompense the Dad before he could lead her away to his cave. Good milch cows were as scarce as good girls—so a wooer hit upon the happy idea, one day, of offering a cow to the "Old Man" for his daughter. The deal was made and cows became, probably, the first money in history.

Since that ancient date most everything that you can think of has been used for money. Carpets, cloth, ornaments, beads, shells, feathers, teeth, hides, tobacco, gophers' tails, woodpeckers' heads, salt, fish hooks, nails, beans, spears, bronze, silver and gold—and later, receipts for gold which did not exist—have all been used for money.

The latter article was the invention of the goldsmith and has yielded greater profits than all other inventions combined. It all came about like this:

Women have always had a fondness for beautiful ornaments. The plainer women—the ones who needed decorating with trinkets—were the ones who received the fewest ornaments. This was because men were the ones who supplied them, and—as contradictory as it may seem—the more beautiful the lady was, the more ornaments she usually received. Rings for her fingers—rings for her toes—rings for her ears—and rings for her nose—bracelets, anklets, tiaras, throatlets, pendants and foibles of yellow gold were hung on her like decorations on a Christmas tree.

Gold was also used to beautify the palaces of the kings, and of the near kings, shrines and temples. It was held in such high esteem that the people actually began to worship it—making gods and goddesses of it. It became the most desired of all substances. Because of the high esteem in which it was held it superseded all of its competitors in the civilized world as a medium of exchange. The value of other goods was measured by the amount of gold for which those goods could be exchanged.

The yellow metal, for convenience sake, and because the gold itself—and not the ornaments which could be made from it—was in demand, was shaped into rings, bars, discs and cubes, usually bearing an imprint of the kingly or princely owner.

Every community, or city, had its king or ruler. These rulers were all eager to increase their hoard of gold. Raiding expeditions were promoted and the weaker tribes, or kingdoms, were looted of the gold which they had accumulated. At times they would become so prosaic and unromantic as to carry on legitimate trade with other communities and obtain the gold in that way—but that was usually too slow and unexciting.

When the king arrived home with the precious stuff, his worries were not over. There were thieves in those days. There were also goldsmiths. The goldsmiths were the manufacturers of the ornaments which the ladies wore, and they always had a considerable amount of the coveted metal on hand. To safeguard their treasures they built strong-rooms on their premises in which to store the gold entrusted to their care.

It was not surprising, then, that the custom grew for the leader, upon his return from his thieving expedition, to leave the hoard of gold which he had obtained, with the goldsmith for safe-keeping. The merchants, too, who had traded profitably with other nations, communities or tribes, as well as other merchants and raiders passing through the city where the goldsmith lived, found it convenient—and usually safe—to leave their gold in the strong-room of the goldsmith.

When the gold was weighed and safely deposited in the strong-room, the goldsmith would give the owner a warehouse receipt for his deposit. These receipts were of various sizes, or for various amounts; some large, others smaller and others still more small. The owner of the gold, when wishing to transact business, would not as a rule take the actual gold out of the strong-room but would merely hand over a receipt for gold which he had in storage.

The goldsmith soon noticed that it was quite unusual for anyone to call for his gold. The receipts, in various amounts, passed from hand to hand instead of the gold itself being transferred. He thought to himself: "Here I am in possession of all this gold and I am still a hard working artisan. It doesn't make sense. Why there are scores of my neighbors who would be glad to pay me interest for the use of this gold which is lying here and never called for.

It is true, the gold is not mine—but it is in my possession, which is all that matters."

The birth of this new idea was promptly followed by action. At first he was very cautious, only loaning a little at a time—and that, on tremendous security. But gradually he became bolder and larger amounts of the gold were loaned.

One day the amount of loan requested was so large that the borrower didn't want to carry the gold away. The gold-smith solved the problem, pronto, by merely suggesting that the borrower be given a receipt for the amount of gold borrowed—or several receipts for various amounts totalling the amount of gold figuring in the transaction. To this the borrower agreed, and off he walked with the receipts, leaving the gold in the strong-room of the goldsmith.

After his client left, the goldsmith smiled broadly. He could have a cake and eat it too. He could lend gold and still have it. The possibilities were well nigh limitless. Others, and still more neighbors, friends, strangers and enemies expressed their desire for additional funds to carry on their businesses—and so long as they could produce sufficient collateral they could borrow as much as they needed—the goldsmith issuing receipts for ten times the amount of gold in his strong-room, *and he not even the owner of that.*

Everything was hunky-dory so long as the real owners of the gold didn't call for it—or so long as the confidence of the people was maintained—or a whispering campaign was not begun; in which case, upon the discovery of the facts, the goldsmith was usually taken out and shot.

In this manner, through the example of the goldsmiths, bank credit entered upon the scene. The practice of issuing receipts—entries in bank ledgers and figures in bank pass books—balancing the borrower's debt against the bank's obligation to pay, and multiplying the obligations to pay by thirty or forty times the amount of money which they (the banks) hold, is a hangover of the goldsmith's racket and is the cause of most of the distress in America and the civilized world today.

As a result of the enormous profits being made by the bankers, the United Nations scheme has been formed to protect them in their franchise and to enable them to exploit the world.

The Bank of Amsterdam, established in 1609 in the City of Amsterdam, was, it seems, the first institution which followed the practice of the goldsmiths under the title of banking. It accepted deposits and gave separate receipts for each deposit of its many depositors, each deposit comprising a new account. The procedure greatly multiplied the number of receipts outstanding. The receipts constituted the medium of exchange in the country.

At first these bankers did not think of or did not intend to follow the practice of the goldsmiths in issuing more receipts than they had in gold, but their avarice soon gained control and that practice was introduced and pursued. The receipts were not covered by gold but by mortgages and property which they believed could be converted into gold on short notice, if necessary.

All went well for a time, but in 1795 the truth leaked out. It was found that the outstanding receipts called for several times the amount of gold which was held by the bank. This discovery caused a panic and a run on the bank resulting in its destruction—because the demand for its gold far exceeded its supply.

The collapse of the Bank of Amsterdam should have been an object lesson to all posterity, but alas, avaricious men again took advantage of the forgetfulness and gullibility of the people and the fraud was revived and perpetuated.

CHAPTER II

THE BANK OF ENGLAND

For centuries, in England, the Christians were taught, and believed, that it was contrary to Christian ethics to loan money at usury, or interest. During those centuries the Church and the State saw eye to eye, for they were practically one and the same. It was, therefore, not only un-Christian, but also illegal to loan money at interest.

The laws of King Alfred, in the Tenth Century, provided that the effects and lands of those who loaned money upon interest should be forfeited to the Crown and the lender should not be buried in consecrated ground. Under Edward the Confessor, in the next Century, it was provided that the usurer should forfeit all his property, be declared an outlaw and banished from England.

During the reign of Henry II, in the Twelfth Century, the estates of usurers were forfeited at their death and their children disinherited. In the Thirteenth Century, King John confiscated and gathered in the wealth of all known usurers. In the Fourteenth Century, the crime of loaning money at interest was made a capital offense, and during the reign of James I, it was held that the taking of usury was no better than taking a man's life.

In view of these facts it is quite understandable how the Jews became, for the most part, the money lenders and the goldsmiths of England. They for some reason had no compunction of conscience on the matter. They lived outside the pale of the teachings of the New Testament and ignored the unmistakable commands of the Old regarding usury. It is true that they had to carry on their business secretly, but carry it on they did.

But so vigorous was the enforcement of law against usury that the money lenders conceived the idea of conspiring together to hoard their money out of circulation. Through this practice that were able to cripple industry and cause depressions. They ultimately became so strongly entrenched, powerful and influential that Parliament found it necessary and expedient to lift the ban against the money lending business and to legalize it. With the legalization of the money lending business (about 1690), the viewpoint of the Christians underwent a change, until they, too, held no antipathy toward the practice and could become a goldsmith money lender as good as the best.

In the year 1693 England's Treasury was empty. In order to carry on her four year old war with France she must have funds. Practically all of the money in the nation had been gathered into the strong-rooms of the money lenders.

Thus it came to pass that King William III, badly in need of money to subdue France and humble proud Louis XIV, appealed to the goldsmiths for a loan of $5,000,000, and the loan was granted.

During this period, toward the end of the Seventeenth Century, a deplorable state of affairs existed in England. The churchmen and the squire ruled the countryside. Territorial magnates monopolized the offices of State. They ruled the House of Lords and the House of Commons. Corruption was general. Goldsmith lenders became fabulously rich on their high rates of interest, and they, of course, pursued the goldsmith policy of loaning up to ten times the amount of money which they actually possessed by issuing receipts for gold which was not in their vaults. Merchants became wealthy through their profits on the slave trade. Trade monopolies flourished and kings and princes shared the plunder they amassed.

Only the common people had no privileges—except those

of doing the work of the nation, fighting its wars and paying taxes and tithes.   They had neither voice nor vote in national affairs.   The agricultural laborer was little better than a serf, and coal miners were chattels, bought and sold with the mine in which they worked.

Those who exploited the poor and made profits out of human misery (for the most part the Society of London), played and drank—and garbed swankily, drove their gilded carriages through the streets of the City.   In London small evidence of the hideous state of affairs in the country, and the world in general, could be seen.

The year 1694 found the war with France still raging and the Treasury of England as empty as Mother Hubbard's cupboard.   King William and his Parliament must obtain more money and there was only one source from whence it might come.   Again they approached the goldsmiths.   This time it was $6,000,000 for which they asked. England had laid the foundation of her national debt the year before; now it was merely a matter of increasing that debt and loading it onto the backs of the taxpayers.

But this time the money lenders were ready for them. During the autumn of 1694 a number of very grave and sagacious men met regularly in, of all places, Mercer's Chapel, in London—to discuss matters of vital importance to England and to the entire world.   Sir John Houblon and William Paterson, with a number of goldsmith colleagues, were busily employed working out the details in connection with the founding of a bank.   When William III asked for more money, they stated the conditions, upon which the money would be loaned to the English Parliament were the following:

1. A Charter must be granted to the lenders for the establishment of a bank—to be known as "The Bank of England"—

and

2. That the bank must be given the right to issue
currency against the gold in its vaults.

On those conditions would the money lenders loan the
English Government the badly needed $6,000,000.

So in the year 1694 the bank of England was established under the leadership of William Patterson and John
Houblon. It was privileged to issue credit against borrowers' collateral in excess of the cash it held on deposit or
actually had to lend, thus creating England's money out of
nothing to the extent of such excess. By 1696 it was circulating about 20 Lbs. Sterling of such paper credit money
against every 1 Lb. Sterling of cash reserves which it
actually had to lend, thus creating 95% of England's
money out of nothing, and William Patterson gleefully
said: "The bank has benefit to the interest on all monies
which it creates out of nothing."

Ever since then, up the centuries, bankers the world over
have so issued paper credit money against borrowers' collateral to varying degree in excess of their cash, most of
the time greatly in excess of the cash they actually had to
lend. Thus have they created the world's money out of
nothing to the precise extent of such excess. They still do
so today. Be the collateral ever so adequate, this IS wholesale legalized counterfeiting, legalized robbery on a gigantic scale.

The banker likes to say that he is merely exchanging
bank credit which is generally acceptable for borrowers'
credit. The borrower's credit which the collateral repre-
sents must however, from every premise of equity, remain
the property of the borrower to the extent that the banker
has issued paper credit money in excess of his cash against
it. It cannot, to this extent, become the banker's property
from ANY premise of equity, to be converted into the
nation's medium of exchange in any form, for this *is*

wholesale legalized counterfeiting when it is done by any privileged private minority, be they private bankers or any other private group. From what premise of equity should they have the enormous predatory privilege to create money out of nothing and to collect interest-tribute thereon? For the collection of interest on money created out of nothing by a privileged private minority is in reality the exaction of tribute.

All this is however being done, and as if this were not enough of predatory privilege, the Federal Reserve conspiracy was enacted. The deceptively misnamed Federal Reserve Banks are private corporations. The Government owns not a single share of stock in the Federal Reserve System. Although the Government was given a modicum of de jure regulatory control over the Federal Reserve Banks, it has preciously little actual de facto control over them. They do as they please. They have the privilege to issue credit greatly in excess of their cash to the Government in exchange for interest bearing bonds, and to private borrowers who can provide them with satisfactory collateral. Thus do they create the nation's money out of nothing to the precise extent of such excess over their cash and collect interest-tribute thereon. How do they get their cash? They were given the further predatory privilege to get their Federal Reserve Notes from the U. S. Bureau of Engraving for the mere cost of printing them, by indirection to be sure, but that is precisely what Federal Reserve Notes cost them. All of the profits of the Federal Reserve System go into their own reserves. The Government does not get one cent of them.

All this adds up to the privilege of UNLIMITED wholesale legalized counterfeiting by a privileged private minority. It is wholesale legalized robbery on the most gigantic scale, far surpassing the sum total of all other forms of robbery, both legalized and illegal, the greatest steal ever conceived by the mortal mind of man.

This greatest of all inequities is the base upon which our banking structure stands. How much longer can it stand? How much longer will it be tolerated? FROM WHAT CONCEIVABLE PREMISE OF EQUITY should any private group or corporation, bank or any other, have the enormous predatory privilege to create money out of nothing while all the rest of us must honestly earn ours? Why the double standard? Are bankers so much better than the rest of us that they should be so *enormously* privileged over all the rest of us?

Whenever robbery, confiscation and/or any other inequity becomes legalized it thereby automatically and inexorably becomes oppressive tyranny, however insidiously indirect and generally imperceptible this may be.

The power to create the world's money, and thereupon to issue it at interest and to control its rate of circulation is the greatest economic power on earth. This power is absolute. It belongs to all the people. To exercise it equitably for the equal benefit of all the people is the supreme prerogative, the highest OBLIGATION, the exclusive right of Government—to the absolute exclusion of all private bankers.—

This greatest of all economic powers, this absolute power has however been usurped by private bankers. With it the international bankers hold the nations in thrall, and these bankers are well aware of this fact, for one of them in this country has recently said: "The prosperity of this country will be precisely what *we* want it to be." And Amschel Rothschild was, in his day, also aware of the absolute power potential inherent in the control of a nation's money, when he said: "Let me issue and control a nation's money and I care not who writes its laws." He should more accurately have said: "Let me *counterfeit* and control a nation's money and I care not who writes its laws." Such is the predatory nature of private banking and the insidiously indirect but absolute power of private bankers. And this absolute power, let us nevermore forget, has been usurped from the people, to whom it properly belongs.

Inasmuch as the very small amount of cash in present day so called deposits has, up the past decades, been issued against borrowers' collateral greatly in excess of any cash then existent, it follows that even this small amount has been created largely out of nothing. We may therefore quite accurately estimate that the bankers had, decades ago, probably less than 1/10% of the present astronomical total of public and private debts to start with. This original less than 1/10% has been pyramided up to the present astronomical total by exercise of the aforesaid UNLIMITED wholesale legalized counterfeiting privileges.

FROM WHAT PREMISE OF EQUITY IS THIS *SO CALLED* DEBT THEN OWED THEM?

Equity demands that this enormous legally stolen wealth, and the usurped issuing power be restored to the people, from whom both were so wrongfully and unconstitutionally taken, to the wholesale injury of mankind at large.

This enormous legally stolen wealth, and the usurped issuing power, this enormous money power is the main, the only really effective weapon of the enemy, the international banking cartel, (for the Bible castigates and identifies Mammon, international money power as the arch enemy of God, Christ and mankind) with which to make and break governments at will, to install and maintain wire pullers behind the scenes on the world stage, to control press, T.V. and radio, to dictate curricula, etc., in short to absolutely rule, exploit and oppress ALL upon this planet. That is the goal.

Until this main weapon is constitutionally stripped from the enemy and restored to the people, to whom it properly belongs, ALL else will be futile. That is the road block which needs most immediately to be removed. ALL other reforms await money reform, await the suppression of this greatest of all inequities and the rectification of this iniquitous money system upon which our social structure stands, or rather totters, and upon which it cannot stand much longer.

CHAPTER III

THE HOUSE OF ROTHSCHILD

In 1750 Amschel Moses Bauer became weary of peddling his wares throughout the country (particularly silver articles of his own manufacture, since he was by trade a gold and silversmith)—and upon his return to Frankfort, Germany, he decided to settle down. He opened a little shop in the Jundenstrasse section and established himself in a permanent business.

Over the door of his goldsmith shop he hung a red shield. From that ingenious man, shop and shield, sprang the most powerful firm of international bankers of the next and present centuries. He, like the goldsmiths who had preceded him, had a strong-room in which he kept his precious metals and that of others who needed the security of a safety deposit vault in which to keep their treasures—and, after the manner of his goldsmith predecessors—practiced the loaning of money at interest on metal and credit which did not belong to him.

Amschel Moses Bauer had a son. He named him Maier Amschel—and he turned out to be a very clever, studious boy. His father decided to make him a rabbi—but in 1754, when Maier was only eleven years of age, his father died. The boy obtained a clerkship in the Oppenheimer Bank in Hanover. Because of his adaptability to the banking business, after a number of years he became a junior partner. Later he returned to Frankfort, bought the little house with the red shield and, assuming the name of Red Shield, established the House of Rothschild (Red Shield).

During the period of his employment with the Bank of

Oppenheimer, but more particularly while he was a partner in the firm, he acquired considerable money. This, with that left him by his father, was sufficient to launch him into business. A rather unholy business it was, to be sure, but very lucrative. It was the business of inducing such German soldiers as he could influence to volunteer and selling them to England to fight its wars with Scotland, France and others —and failing to obtain volunteers, he would kidnap the men. In 1787, for example, he supplied England with 12,000 men and received in payment, 80,000 pounds sterling. These men virtually became slaves. Such sales were numerous year after year—and thus was the foundation of the Rothschild great fortune laid.

Maier Amschel (Bauer) Rothschild had five sons. These sons, through their natural, if unscrupulous, genius—and through the tutorship of their adroit father—became Captains of High Finance in all the Nations of Europe. So powerful did the combination become that they could overthrow governments and dethrone kings. They were international bankers with a vengeance.

Nathan Rothchild became the greatest financial wizard of his, or probably any other, generation. He was born in 1777 and at the age of 21 went to England with 20,000 pounds which suddenly grew to 60,000 pounds. A part of his father's wealth was also accessible to him. He became interested in national and international investments.

Napoleon was over-running Europe and was a real threat to the thrones of England and Germany. France had been subdued and Louis XVIII could only pray that Napoleon's power would be broken in order that he might take the throne to which he was then heir. Nathan Rothschild was undecided as to the outcome of the war. If he was to profit, regardless of which armies were victorious, he must be in a position to obtain authoritative information before the

English Parliament or the rank and file of the people were in possession of it.

The decisive battle of the campaign was about to be fought—The Battle of Waterloo. Nathan hurried to Paris and secured a palace adjoining that of Louis XVIII. The day of the momentous battle dawned and Nathan occupied a position at a window through which he could look right into the palace of the aspirant to the throne.

In the afternoon a dust begrimed messenger arrived on a foaming steed. He was admitted at once into the palace of the King. The message which he bore caused Louis to become jubilant. Nathan knew that Wellington had been victorious and that Napoleon had suffered his downfall.

He made his decision and acted with great haste.

Hurrying to the docks he hired a' sailor for 2000 pounds to take him, during a raging storm at the peril of their lives, across the English Channel.

Upon his arrival in England he found the Nation in despair. A little bird had brought the word that Wellington had been defeated at Waterloo and that Napoleon was ready to launch his campaign against England and take the throne. Panic was rampant. The bottom dropped out of values. English pounds sterling could be bought for a song or a shilling. That little bird (a carrier pigeon) had been released by a confederate of Nathan as soon as Wellington's victory was certain, and to its leg was tied the lie. Nathan Rothschild scooped up the pounds, shillings and sixpence of England at a fraction of their value. It is a mystery how he escaped assassination when the truth was known—but such is the luck of bankers and the power of money, however obtained. It is usually their opponents who meet with timely and fortuitous death.

Nathan Rothschild, after the haul, found it possible to loan England, because of the magnanimity of his noble

heart, 18,000,000 pounds—and to Prussia he loaned 5,-
000,000 pounds—to repair the damages of war.

All four of Nathan's brothers indulged in much the same
brand of banking policy. Their Al Capone system was to
juggle a government into a position of distress and then
squeeze it as tightly as the case would permit, leaving a
tax-burdened and impoverished populace to bear the heavy
weight of taxes occasioned by their exploitation.

Nathan Rothschild died in 1836, twenty years after the
Rothschild clan had gained control of the Bank of England.

His son, Lionel, was elected to the British Parliament,
where he wielded a great influence, but not in the interests
of the common people. His central office he maintained in
Frankfort in the house of the Red Shield. Even to this day
the Rothschilds are dominant figures in the financial and
banking world.

The story of the successful attempt of the Rothschilds to
extend their financial kingdom to America and to gain control of this, our Nation, will be told in succeeding chapters.

CHAPTER IV

The Bankers Invade the Colonies

When the Pilgrims landed at Plymouth to found the first New England Colony, several other Colonies had already been established in America. In 1565 the Spaniards had settled in St. Augustine, Florida. The French had already established a Colony at Port Royal in Nova Scotia in 1605. Two years later the London Company had established a Colony at Jamestown, Virginia. In 1614 Dutch fur traders began to frequent Manhattan Island with the result that New Amsterdam, later named New York, took its place on the map.

The arrival of the *Mayflower*, with its load of robust souls, at Plymouth, Massachusetts, December 21st, 1620, proved to be the first mighty vanguard of a great multitude to arrive from across the sea. English immigration, on a large scale, followed in 1630, resulting in the establishment of the Colonies of Maine, Connecticut, New Haven, Rhode Island and New Hampshire. The influx of immigrants from the other nations, who had begun to settle in the new land, was also accelerated.

Little money, during these first years of colonization, was seen in America. The settlers bartered their produce and goods with each other. But after the first few hardy pioneers had hewed out their homes and cleared the forests for their new fields, men of considerable means joined the steady procession westward from the Old World. They brought gold and silver coin and this was used to facilitate trade between the people comprising the various Colonies, and also the trade between the Colonies themselves.

Indian Wampum, black and white shells, which represented certain values among the Indians, also found its way into the hands of the Whites, who soon learned that they could use it as a medium of exchange very satisfactorily. Later Wampum became legal tender in some of the States. The Colonies also stamped gold and silver coins and put them in circulation.

It became apparent, however, after a time, that trade was being hindered because of insufficient money—or something to use for money. Thus it came about that a circulating medium—called "Colonial Scrip"—was printed by the Governors of the various Colonies. With this release of adequate purchasing power great prosperity came to the Colonies since there was an abundance of produce and goods available.

The Nations of Europe, from which the colonists had come, were repeatedly at war. These wars spread to America so that we find the various Colonies frequently at war with each other. The Indians, also, were induced to become involved in these wars. The colonists from England, supported by soldiers from across the sea, finally succeeded in vanquishing their foes. By the treaty of Paris in 1763 England gained possession of all the land East of the Mississippi from Hudson Bay to the Gulf of Mexico. The stage was set for momentary invasion.

About this time Benjamin Franklin made a visit to England. While there he was asked how he accounted for the prosperous condition of the Colonies. His reply was: "That is simple. It is only because in the Colonies we issue our own money. It is called 'Colonial Scrip'—and we issue it in the proper proportion to the demands of trade and industry." (See Senate Document No. 23, page 98, by Robert L Owen, Former Chairman, Committee on Banking and Currency, United States Senate.)

Robert L. Owen continues: "It was not very long until

this information was brought to the Rothschild's bank, and they saw that here was a Nation ready to be exploited; here was a Nation that had been setting up an example that they could issue their own money in place of the money coming through the banks. The Rothschild Bank caused a Bill to be introduced in the English Parliament, therefore, which provided that no Colony of England could issue its own money. They had to use English money. Consequently the Colonies were compelled to discard their 'Scrip' and mortgage themselves to the Bank of England in order to get money. For the first time in the history of the United States our money began to be based on debt.

"Benjamin Franklin stated that in one year from that date the streets of the Colonies were filled with the unemployed, because when England exchanged with them she gave them only half as many units in payment in borrowed money from the Rothschild Bank as they had in 'Scrip'. In other words, their circulating medium was reduced fifty per cent, and everyone became unemployed, according to Benjamin Franklin's own statement."

Continuing the quote from Senate Document No. 23: "Mr. Franklin went further than that. He said that this was the original cause of the Revolutionary War. In his own language: *'The Colonies would gladly have borne the little tax on tea and other matters had it not been that England took away from the Colonies their money, which created unemployment and dissatisfaction'* "

It was Maier Amschel Rothschild who had said, in 1790, "Permit me to issue and control the money of a nation and I care not who writes its laws." In the enactment of this law by the English Parliament in 1764 (at the instigation of the Rothschilds), we have a perfect illustration of the truthfulness of the Rothschild boast.

On April 19th, 1775, the first armed clashes of the Revolution against Bankerism took place at Lexington and Concord.   On May 10th the Second Continental Congress assembled at Philadelphia.   George Washington was placed at the head of Naval and Military affairs and took command at Cambridge. On July 4th of the next year Congress adopted the Declaration of Independence.

For seven years the War continued.   Finally, however, Cornwallis and his whole army, including what were left of the 16,000 Hessian soldiers supplied by the Rothschilds to keep America in bonds, was captured at Yorktown and surrendered to George Washington, October 19th, 1781.   On September 3rd, 1783, by the Peace of Paris, the Independence of the United States was recognized.

In 1786 fifty-five delegates from the majority of the States met to formulate a plan whereby the States would be enabled to live amicably with each other, and to outline a policy to facilitate trade and industry.   The delegates labored for four months over the problems presented, the principal one being as to how the Northern States with paid labor, could compete with the Southern States with free labor.   It appeared doubtful, for a time, that an agreement could be arrived at and a unified Nation established.   Both sides made compromises.   The Constitution, minus the Bill of Rights, was the result.

A Constitutional Convention was called for the next year, 1787, at Philadelphia.   At that Convention the Constitution of the United States, which embodied a provision for its amendment, was adopted by a majority of the States, with few alterations.

Not forgetful of the bitter experiences through which the Country had passed because of the act of the English Parliament by which the Colonies were denied the privilege of creating their own purchasing power—and were forced to accept banker-created, interest bearing, Bank of England money—the Founding Fathers made sure that provisions were made by the Constitution for an honest and debt free money system.   Thus, in spite of the strenuous opposition of banker-minded delegates to the Convention, Article 1, Section 8, Paragraph 5 was drafted and adopted, with the rest of the Constitution.   It is still an important, though disregarded, Article of the Constitution.

Article 1, Section 8, Paragraph 5, states, in part: *"Congress shall have power to coin money and regulate the value thereof."* It is most evident that by this provision, Congress alone should be the money-creating agency of the Nation. That the term, "coin money," included the printing of currency was later established by at least eight decisions of the Supreme Court of the United States.

Although the Constitution is regarded by the citizens of the United States as being a well nigh sacred document, and all laws are supposedly made to conform to its provisions, yet, because of the entrenched power and intrigue of the bankers, Article 1, Section 8, Paragraph 5 has been violated, almost continuously, since the adoption of the Constitution. *The bankers are the money-creators of the Nation.*   To this fact can be traced the cause of every depression, every bank failure, our staggering National debt and the poverty of the vast majority of our citizens, and the slow starvation of one-third of our population, while vast amounts of the produce of the Nation are being intentionally destroyed.

CHAPTER V

A FREE NATION IN BONDS

Wars are the "happy hunting grounds" of the bankers. While our patriotic soldiers were heroically fighting to break the power of the bankers and gain national as well as economic independence, a supposed patriot—Alexander Hamilton—was busily engaged planning a double-cross. A hireling of the Bank of England, he proposed, in 1780, the establishment of a Federal Bank, owned by private interests, with a capital of $12,000,000—$10,000,000 of the amount to be supplied by the Bank of England. The remaining $2,000,000 was to be subscribed by wealthy people of America.

In 1783 the Bank of America was organized by Alexander Hamilton and Robert Morris, front men of the racketeers behind the scenes. As Superintendent of Finance for the Continental Congress, Morris frisked the United States Treasury of its last dollar remaining after the seven years of war (about $250,000), and put it in the Bank's capital stock.

The secret leaked out that this supposedly American institution was, in reality, a branch of the Bank of England, and that that bank's policy of perpetuating the goldsmith's racket of issuing receipts—or promises to deliver gold—for about ten times the amount they had in gold or real money, and—of course—charging interest on their promises to deliver receipts (now known as bank notes) was to be the policy of the newly established Bank of America.

The knowledge of this fact precipitated prolonged and bitter controversy. Thomas Jefferson, Andrew Jackson,

John Adams, James Madison and Benjamin Franklin led the assault against the avaricious foe. They knew that were the monopolistic control of the Nation's money to pass, once more, into the hands of the Bank of England, the gaining of National Independence would have been accomplished in vain, for that which the money powers of England had lost through revolution would ultimately be returned to them through the process of mortgage and foreclosure. A charter was refused the proposed bank.

In 1791 death removed the mighty defender of the people's rights, Benjamin Franklin, and the logical protests of the other able statesmen were swept aside by the surge of bankers' gold. In 1791 Congress granted the exclusive privilege of grinding out currency based on public and private debts to Alexander Hamilton—who had by that time inveigled his way into the Office of the Treasury—and to his money manipulating cohorts, by chartering their bank.

The arguments of the bankers' mouthpieces that money issued by Congress on the credit of the Nation would be valueless; that only money issued by a bank and which paid the bankers interest had any value (although the money thus issued amounted to many times the amount of gold, or assets which supported it) were heeded by a public who were soon to fall prey to the exploitation of those who professed to be their benefactors.

The Bank of the United States, with its 90 branches, became a reality. With the establishment of the Bank, and the granting of its charter, Alexander Hamilton resigned from the Office of Secretary of the Treasury, to devote all his time to the exploitation of the Nation. He later was killed in a duel with Aaron Burr, but not over the issue for which he deserved to die a traitor's death.

Of the $35,000,000 capitalization of the Bank, $28,000,-000 were provided by European bankers, principally the Rothschilds, leaving $7,000,000 to be subscribed by Americans. From this fact it is not difficult to conclude by whom the financial interests of the Nation were controlled.

Thus the stage was set for the International Bankers to retake America, through the simple process of extending and contracting credit; by first providing ample money and then creating a money stringency; by loaning money on first mortgages and then foreclosing the mortgagors out of their possessions; and by gathering interest on every dollar in circulation in the Nation.

Of the perpetuation of this fraud on America many of our ablest Statesmen have left on record their views on the matter. John Adams, in writing to Thomas Jefferson in 1787, said: "All the perplexities, confusion and distress in America arises, not from the defects of the Constitution or Confederation—not from want of honor or virtue, so much as from down right ignorance of the nature of coin, credit and circulation."

Thomas Jefferson said: *"I believe that banking institutions are more dangerous to our liberties than standing armies. Already they have raised up a money aristocracy that has set the government at defiance. The issuing power should be taken from the banks and restored to the people to whom it properly belongs."*

Andrew Jackson said: "If Congress has a right under the Constitution to issue paper money, it was given them to be used by themselves, not to be delegated to individuals or corporations."

Quotations from other Statesmen will follow in their proper sequence.

The charter of the Bank of the United States was for twenty years, expiring in 1811. When its officers applied for a renewal of the charter, Congress, realizing the hideous mistake of granting a private institution such tremendous powers, refused to renew the charter.

At a later date President Andrew Jackson made good

his threat when he told the Bankers to their faces: *"You are a den of vipers and thieves. I intend to rout you out, and by the eternal God, I will rout you out."*

The English Parliament, always subservient to the Bank of England (which, like all other banking institutions, works behind the scenes, avoiding the divulgence of the fact that, in reality, the object of most wars is to further the bankers' interests, stating other grievances as the causes), launched the War of 1812. By this War it was expected that America would become impoverished and would be forced to come on her knees to the Bank of England for funds. The condition upon which money would be supplied would be the renewal of the charter of their subsidiary bank, The Bank of the United States.

Their plan worked. Their dreams came true. A subservient and bribed Congress granted a renewal of the charter in 1816. The tentacles of the octopus, which had been severed, were quickly joined and healed and became stronger than ever, and soon had a still firmer grip upon the fair form of Miss America.

CHAPTER VI

More Rothschild Strategy

By 1857 the grip of the Rothschilds was so powerful in America, and their greed so great, that they planned the actual possession of the Nation. It came about in the following manner. The marriage of Lenora, daughter of Lionel Rothschild, to her cousin, Alfonso of Paris, was the occasion which brought the members of the family, and other great personages, together in London.

Disraeli, the noted English Statesman, was there and, according to at least one historian, made a most audacious speech, a part of which, it is reported, was as follows:

"Under this roof are the heads of the family of Rothschild, a name famous in every capital in Europe and every division of the globe. If you like we shall divide the United States into two parts, one for you, James, and one for you, Lionel. Napoleon will do exactly, and all that I shall advise him, and to Bismarck will be suggested such an intoxicating program as to make him our abject slave."

Since "Deeds speak louder than words," it is a matter of small consequence whether Disraeli uttered these words, or others attributed to him by other historians. Nor is it a matter of great importance whether it was at that wedding banquet, or on some other occasion, that the plot was laid, by the internationalists, to repossess, divide, exploit and plunder the United States. Subsequent events clearly indicate that the plot was planned and put into effect. Judah P. Benjamin, a Rothschild relative, it is reported, was appointed, by the Rothschilds, professional agitator and campaign strategist in America. The Civil War, which all but split the Union, became a fact.

Napoleon III was persuaded that he could greatly increase the power and wealth of France by extending his empire to Mexico. England was assured that the Northern States could be made a Colony once more.

The slave problem was, as we have seen, an economic problem. The Civil War was an economic war—as most all wars are. The Northern States had voluntarily freed their slaves and found, as the Founding Fathers feared, that they could not compete, industrially and economically, with the southern states which employed slave labor. Harriet Beecher Stowe's book, "Uncle Tom's Cabin," brought the nation face to face with the slave issue.

Abraham Lincoln was a true Statesman—a humanitarian and an idealist. He was profoundly sincere in his desire to help the colored people by freeing them from their frequently cruel masters. He was also profoundly concerned about America's future, realizing, as he said: "No nation can long endure half free and half slave."

Rothschild money flowed into the South, and a loan of 201,500,000 francs was granted by them to Napoleon for his Mexican campaign. In 1863 the Confederacy required assistance. Napoleon was offered Texas and Louisiana in exchange for French intervention against the Northern States. When the Czar of Russia, Alexander II, heard of this he notified France and England that should they extend military aid to the South that it would be regarded as a declaration of war against Russia. To strengthen his statement he sent warships to New York and San Francisco and placed them at Lincoln's disposal.

But the North was facing extreme difficulty in financing the war. The interest rate set by the banks was 28%.

At the outset it was expected that the conflict would last but a few months, which probably would have been the case

had the European nations, at the instigation of the Rothschilds, not come to the assistance of the South.

In his extremity Lincoln did a very wise thing. He turned
to the Constitution of the United States—and sure enough,
there he found the solution to the nation's financial problem.

The bankers and their hirelings, of course, fought Lincoln
bitterly when he declared his intention to issue money according to the provisions of the Constitution. They disap-
proved of the idea of creating money which did not pay
them interest.

Lincoln held his ground.   Article 1, Section 8, Paragraph
5 was sufficient authority for him to disregard the power-
fully entrenched bankers. He did not believe that the Constitution meant *"Banker"* where it states: *"Congress"* shall
have power to coin money—." So, in spite of the greedy
bankers' protests he caused to have printed, in the Bureau
of Printing and Engraving a total of $450,000,000 of hon-
est money, Constitutionally created on the credit of the
nation.

The outraged bankers got busy. They caused a Bill to be
passed through Congress which ruled that "Lincoln Greenbacks"—as the United States Notes were, in derision, called
—would not be accepted in payment of interest on government bonds nor for import duties. In this way they caused
them to become almost worthless, because they could refuse
to accept them, unless at a discount.

The bankers beat the value of the "Greenbacks" down to
about 30 cents on the dollar, and then bought them in—the
King Midas touch was applied and they were then used, at
face value, to buy Government Bonds at par, a neat profit
of 70 cents on the dollar accruing to the Shylocks.

The patriotic, Constitutional act of President Lincoln in
issuing "Greenbacks" caused a furor in the banking circles
of the world. Regarding this policy, an editorial in the

London Times (which, like most other metropolitan papers, was dominated by the banking interests) said:

"If this mischievous financial policy, which has its origin in the North American Republic, shall become endurated down to a fixture, then that Government will furnish its own money without cost. It will pay off its debts and be without debt. It will have all the money necessary to carry on its commerce. It will become prosperous without precedent in the history of the world. The brains and the wealth of all countries will go to North America. *That government must be destroyed or it will destroy every monarchy on the globe.*"

Hurriedly the bankers held a convention in Washington. They evidently found many vulnerable Senators and Congressmen there. The National Bank Act of 1863 was drafted. There were willing hands across the sea to assist them in fighting to gain control of the Nation's money. From London come "The Hazard Circular"—to be distributed among the banking fraternity here. It reads as follows:

"Slavery is likely to be abolished by the war power. This I and my European friends are in favor of, for slavery is but the owning of labor and carries with it the care of the laborers, while the European plan, led on by England, is that *capital shall control labor by controlling wages.*

"The great debt that Capitalists will see to it is made out of the war must be used to control the value of money. To accomplish this *government bonds must be used as a banking basis.* We are now waiting for the Secretary of the Treasury of the United States to make that recommendation.

"It will not do to allow greenbacks, as they are called, to circulate as money for any length of time as we cannot control that. But we can control the bonds and through them the banking issues."

The National Bank Act became law by an act of a servile Congress over President Lincoln's strong protest.

Two very revealing letters, which show how a banker's mind works, and which also indicate the enormity of their well laid plot against America through the National Banking Act, read as follows:

"ROTHSCHILD BROTHERS, BANKERS

London, June 25, 1863

Messrs. Ikelheimer, Morton and Vandergould,
No. 3, Wall St.,
New York, U. S. A.
Dear Sirs:

A Mr. John Sherman has written us from a town in Ohio, U.S.A., as to the profit that may be made in the National Banking business, under a recent act of your Congress; a copy of this act accompanies this letter.

Apparently this act has been drawn up on the plan formulated here by the *British Bankers Association*, and by that Asociation recommended to our American friends, as one that, if enacted into law, *would prove highly profitable to the banking fraternity throughout the world.*

Mr. Sherman declares that there has never been such an opportunity for *capitalists to accumulate money* as that presented by this act. It gives the National Bank almost complete control of the National finance. 'The few who understand the system,' he says, 'will either be so interested in its profits, or so dependent on its favors that there will be no opposition from that class, while, on the other hand, the great body of people, *mentally incapable of comprehending* the tremendous advantages that Capital derives from the system, will bear its burden without complaint, and perhaps without even suspecting that the system is inimical to their interests   .   .   .'

Your respectful servants,
ROTHSCHILD BROTHERS."

"NEW YORK CITY
July 6, 1863

Messrs. Rothschild Brothers,
London, England.
Dear Sirs:

We beg to acknowledge receipt of your letter of June 25, in which you refer to a communication received of Honorable John Sherman of Ohio, with reference to the advantages and profits of an American investment under the provisions of the National Banking Act.

Mr. Sherman possesses in a marked degree the distinguishing characteristics of a successful financier. His temperament is such that *whatever his feeling may be they never cause him to lose sight of the main chance.*

He is young, shrewd and ambitious. He has fixed his eyes upon the Presidency of the United States and is already a member of Congress (he has financial ambitions, too). He rightfully thinks that he has everything to gain by being friendly with men and institutions having large financial resources, and *which at times are not too particular in their methods,* either of obtaining government aid, or protecting themselves against unfriendly legislation.

As to the organization of the National Bank here and the nature and profits of such investments we beg leave to refer to our printed circulars enclosed herein, viz:

'Any number of persons not less than five may organize a National Banking Corporation.

'Except in cities having 6000 inhabitants or less, a National Bank cannot have less than $1,000,000 capital.

'They are *private corporations organized for private gain,* and select their own officers and employees.

'They are not subject to control of State Laws, except as Congress may from time to time provide.

'They may receive deposits and loan the same for their

own benefit. They can buy and sell bonds and discount paper and do a general banking business.

. 'To start a National Bank on the scale of $1,000,000 will require purchase of that amount (par value) of U.S. Government Bonds.

'U. S. Government Bonds *can now be purchased at 50%* discount, so that a bank of $1,000,000 capital can be started at this time for *only $500,000.*

'These bonds must be deposited in the U. S. Treasury at Washinton as security for the National Bank currency, *that will be furnished by the government to the bank.*

'The United States Government will pay 6% interest on the bonds in gold, the interest being paid semi-annually. It will be seen that at the present price of bonds the interest paid by *the government itself is 12% in gold on all money invested.*

'The U. S. Government on having the bonds aforesaid deposited with the Treasurer, on the strength of such security will furnish National currency to the bank depositing the bonds, at an annual interest of *only one per cent per annum.*

'The currency is printed by the U. S. Government in a form so like greenbacks, that the people do not detect the difference. *Although the currency is but a promise of the bank to pay.*

'The demand for money is so great that this money can be readily loaned to the people across the counter of the bank *at a discount at the rate of 10%* at thirty to sixty days time, *making it about 12% interest on the currency.*

'The interest on the bonds, plus the interest on the currency which the bonds, plus incidentals of the business, ought to make the gross earnings of the bank amount to from 28% to 33 1/3%.

'National Banks are privileged to *increase and contract their currency at will,* and of course, can grant or withhold loans as they may see fit.   As the banks have a National organization and can easily act together *in withholding loans or extending them,* it follows that they can by united action in *refusing to make loans cause a stringency in the money market, and in a single week or even a single day cause a decline in all products of the country.*

'National Banks pay no taxes on their bonds, *nor on their capital, nor on their deposits.'*

Requesting that you will regard this as strictly confidential . . .

Most respectfully yours,
IKELHEIMER, MORTON AND VANDERGOULD."

From the foregoing letters it is quite obvious that by the provisions of the National Banking Act there was placed in the hands of the bankers the power not only to get money for nothing, with which to start a bank, but also the power to create propitious conditions whereby rich harvests could be reaped on the stock market as well as through foreclosing upon the real property placed in their hands by those who borrowed money or credit from the bankers.

Abraham Lincoln

"I see in the near future a crisis approaching that unnerves me and causes me to tremble for the safety of my Country; corporations have been enthroned, an era of corruption in high places will follow, and the money power of the Country will endeavor to prolong its reign by working upon the prejudices of the people, until the wealth is aggregated in a few hands, and the Republic is destroyed."

Shortly after making that prophetic statement (which has been all but fulfilled) Abraham Lincoln was shot to death one evening in a darkened theatre—and the people of the Nation still wonder who instigated his assassination.   It is.

passing strange, however, that a coded message was found in the trunk of Booth, the assassin, the key to which was discovered in Judah P. Benjamin's possession. Benjamin, you will remember, was the Civil War campaign strategist for the House of Rothschild.

Salmon P. Chase

Secretary of the Treasury, 1861-1864

"My agency in promoting the passage of the National Banking Act was the greatest financial mistake of my life. It has built up a monopoly which affects every interest in the Country. It should be repealed but before that can be accomplished, *the people will be arrayed on one side and the banks on the other*, in a contest such as we have never seen before in this country."

Horace Greeley

"While boasting of our noble deeds, we are careful to conceal the ugly fact that by an iniquitous money system we have nationalized a system of oppression, which, though more refined, is not less cruel than the old system of chattel slavery,"

James A. Garfield

"Whoever controls the volume of money in any country is absolute master of industry and commerce."

Now that the results of allowing the absolute control of the Nation's money, together with its creation, to pass into the hands of a group of unscrupulous, avaricious, unpatriotic men are history, we can understand why the men whom we have quoted looked with apprehension upon the vicious act which had been, by intrigue, subtlety and bribery made a law on the statute books of the Nation.   Let us see if their misgivings were well founded.

In 1866 there were $1,906,687,770 in currency in the Nation, or $50.46 per capita.   The next year the work of contracting the Nation's money was begun by the money powers with the destruction of over $86,000,000.   This withdrawal of money from circulation caused 2,386 business failures.

The next year $473,000,000 was withdrawn from circulation resulting in 2,608 business failures with a loss of $63,774,000. The destruction of money continued at about this rate for ten more hideous years, reducing the currency in the Nation by $1,301,436,000, leaving but $605, 251,770 to circulate. This brought the per capita currency down to $14.60 and resulted in a total of 56,446 business failures with a total loss of $2,245,105,000.

The majority of the losses sustained were represented by mortgage foreclosures.   Thus it can be seen how the real wealth of the Nation was rapidly passing into the hands of the bankers.   The Rothschilds failed in their attempt to divide the Nation between them by force of arms, but the tactics employed were fully as successful.   It must not be forgotten that they gained control of the bank of England in 1816 and the fact not overlooked that the banking system in America was but a branch of the English institution, and was largely under Rothschild domination.   There is plenty of evidence pointing to the fact that the situation has not materially changed.

Another reason for the banker's program of contracting the circulating medium was that they intended to keep the laboring man impoverished and thus more servile.   About this time the following article appeared in the *New York World,* which throws considerable light on the dark subject:

"American labor must make up its mind henceforth

not to be so much better off than European labor.   Men must be content to work for less wages. In this way *the working man will be nearer that station in life to which it has pleased God to call him."*

The parasitical banking fraternity, which makes the largest profits of any class of business, also pays the lowest wages to their employees.   They like to see three hundred men clamoring for every job and their dominated and co-operative industrial magnates hold no antipathy towards seeing long lines of half starved men at their factory gates, seeking employment, each morning.

That causes those who have a job to feel quite grateful to their employers for being allowed to work, no matter what the abuse or how small the pay.   "That all men are created equal," is a beautiful, but it seems, usually forgotten fact.

The American Banking System, under the National Banking Act, working hand in glove with the Bank of England, were not yet satisfied with their accomplishments in the United States.   They had only begun their hideous program of impoverishing the Nation for their own enrichment. Still darker years were soon to follow.

CHAPTER VII

SILVER DEMONETIZED

During the period in which the bankers, by the powers given them by the National Banking Act of 1863, were collapsing the currency of the Nation from $50.46 per capita down to $14.60, they were scheming another method whereby the people could be further impoverished and the bankers' control strengthened.

In 1816, in England, the Rothschilds had succeeded in having silver demonetized as a base upon which currency could be issued. Gold was made the only base for the issuance of paper money. They and their stooges in America decided, in 1872, to have silver demonetized in the United States. This was desirable to the Rothschilds because England had very little silver, but much gold, while America had much silver and very little gold. The bankers on both sides of the Atlantic knew that so long as currency was based on silver in America they could not obtain absolute control of the money system in this Nation.

They laid their plans in a most subtle manner. They sent paid emissaries to America with vast amounts of money with which to bribe the right persons in Congress. In 1873, a harmless looking Bill, entitled, "A Bill to Reform Coinage and Mint Laws," was introduced. It was a voluminous document. Much verbiage concealed the meaning of its contents. The title itself, as intended, was most misleading.

The Bill was sponsored by Senator John Sherman, who—you will remember—figured in a banker's letter in the preceding chapter, and by Congressman Samuel Hooper. According to the Congressional Record, Senator Sherman said:

"I rise for the purpose of moving the Senate to proceed to the consideration of the Mint Bill. I will state that this Bill will probably not consume any more time than it takes to read it. It passed the Senate two years ago, after a dull debate. It was taken up in the present house and passed there. It is a matter of vital interest to the government, and I am informed it should pass promptly."

After a short debate, in which Sherman assured the Representatives that the Bill only affected the manner in which silver should be coined in the government mint, it was passed without a dissenting vote. It was not until three years later that the full import of the bill was realized. It *proved to be a camouflaged bill to demonetize silver* so that the currency in the Nation could be further contracted—and the bankers gain more complete control of our money system. It was, perhaps, the greatest fraud ever perpetrated on Americans, the far reaching results of which we will consider shortly.

General Grant, who, as President, signed the Bill, stated, after the fraud had been discovered, that he had signed the document without reading it on the representation that it was merely a bill to reform coinage and mint laws, and had no intimation that it demonetized silver. According to the Congressional Record, none but the members of the Committee which introduced the Bill understood its meaning.

To what power, or influence, was the Committee subjected that those composing it should become traitors to the high office they held and to the people whom they represented?

Ernest Seyd—a supposed authority on the coining of money, and a representative of the Bank of England—was sent by that Bank in the winter of 1872-73, with 100,000 pounds sterling ($500,000) in his pocket, and the authority to draw on the Bank for as much more as was required to accomplish the Bank's objective. He was invited to sit with the Committee and to offer his assistance in the drafting of the Bill "To Reform Coinage and Mint Laws."

According to his own statement, made to his friend, Mr. Frederick A. Luckenbach, of Denver, Colorado—who has, under oath, given us the story,—he said: "I saw the Committee of the House and Senate and *paid the money* and stayed in America until I knew the measure was safe."

Congressman Samuel Hooper, when introducing the Bill in the House on April 9, 1872, stated: "Mr. Ernest Seyd, of London, a distinguished writer, who has given great attention to the subject of mints and coinage, after examining the first draft of the Bill, furnished many valuable suggestions which have been incorporated in the Bill." (Congressional Globe, April 9, 1872.)

Thus we see that this representative of Rothschild's Bank —the Bank of England—Mr. Ernest Seyd, did not only supply the cash motive for this Nation's representatives to sell the Nation down the river, but he also furnished a liberal portion of craftiness while the Bill was being drafted. To even the casual observer it is quite obvious that the banking institutions of America are but subsidiary branches of the notorious Bank of England and that the combined unscrupulous, unpatriotic and undemocratic banking fraternity, operating as they do—outside and above the law—are masters of industry, trade and commerce, and lords of the universe.

When the people's representatives got around to reading the enacted Bill to Reform Coinage and Mint Laws, they found that the "Crime of 1873" had been committed. Silver had been demonetized in America—and with what tragic results! It was not until 1878 that the bankers had the nerve to show their hand by beginning to exercise their privileges under the Act—the destruction of money—but when they began, they prosecuted their maniacal job with Satanic zeal.

In 1878 the per capita currency in circulation was withdrawn and destroyed from $14.60 down to $11.23. This resulted in 10,478 business failures and multitudinous property foreclosures. In 1879 the issuance of coin by Congress brought the circulating medium up to $12.65, which reduced the failures from the preceding year to 6,658. But in 1882 the hideous program of bringing the Nation to its knees so that it could be delivered into the hands of the money-creating, interest-taking, mortgage-foreclosing Shylocks was renewed and prosecuted with fiendish determination and skill.

During the next five years (1882-1887), the per capita money in circulation was reduced from a meagre $12.65 to $6.67. During the 14 years in which money was being destroyed under the Bill "To Reform Coinage and Mint Laws," (1878-1892), there were no fewer than 148,703 business failures in the Nation—an average of 9,986 annually, with the resultant profits to the Bankers, through the acquiring of those properties, together with a proportionately greater number of farms and homes.

Although business was ham-strung by the shortage of money, high interest rates and high taxes, and although unemployment was general, with the wages of the few who worked extremely low, and hours long, the avaricious money masters were not yet satisfied. Their object then was the same as now—*the absolute control of the Nation.*

On March 11, 1893, the American Bankers' Association issued its famous (or infamous) *panic circular* of 1893. It was addressed to all bankers and read as follows:

"Dear Sir:
The interest of the National Banks requires immediate financial legislation by Congress. Silver certificates and

Treasury notes must be retired, and National Bank notes upon a gold basis made the only money. This will require the authorization of new bonds in the amount of $500,000,-000 to $1,000,000,000, as the basis of circulation. *You will at once retire one-third of your circulation and call one-half your patrons—especially among influential business men.* The life of the National Banks, as fixed and safe investments, depends upon immediate action *as there is an increasing sentiment in favor of government legal tender notes and silver coinage."*

The command was obeyed immediately and implicitly. Loans were called. *The ordered money stringency was created* and the "Panic of 1893" was on. The great Commoner and Statesman, William Jennings Bryan, fought desperately for the free coinage of silver at a ratio of sixteen ounces of silver to one of gold—but the people, under the influence of their bankers (whom they foolishly did not suspect of treason), refused to be enlightened on the *money racket.* His was a voice "Crying in the wilderness," and he was crucified on a *"cross of gold."*

From Judge P. E. Gardner's book, "Our Money System" —which contains a wealth of valuable information—I quote the following:

.."*The money trust knows no God but Mammon. It declares allegiance to no country. It cares not who are elected to office so long as it creates the money and regulates the value thereof."*

CHAPTER VIII

The Federal Reserve

In 1913, and even prior to that year, the munitions manufacturers, the war lords and the international bankers,
knew that war in Europe was imminent. They knew this
because they, in combination, are the principal creators of
war—as well as the profiteers from wars.

The Bank of England, with its subsidiary banks in America (under the domination of J. P. Morgan), the Bank of
France and the Reichbank of Germany—composed an inter-
locking and co-operative banking system, the main objective
of which was the exploitation of the people. It matters
little to them whether their profits are made by the dispos-
session of their mortgaged victims or from the blowing up
of the accumulated wealth of the nations while prosecuting
their program of legalized murder on a world-wide scale.

It is passing strange that munitions factories are not the
objects of attack, in time of war, until you know that the
bankers own and control the munitions factories—even those
of their enemies. Why destroy the source of devastation
when it yields such handsome profits? Why so speedily
terminate the slaughter, as the destruction of the enemy's
munitions factories and arsenals would bring about, so long
as money can be created with a fountain pen by the bankers
and loaned to the people at interest, by which process, they-
—the people—pay for the war?

Battleships, airplanes, field guns, fortifications and the
uniforms of the fighting men, bought and paid for at tremendous profits with money borrowed on government bonds
from the money creating, interest gathering International

Bankers, are destroyed wholesale—but not so the banker-owned munitions factories.   Their destruction would constitute a direct loss to them and would hamper their gathering of profits through the continuance of the war.

A Sidelight on the Internationalist

"Arms and the men," a booklet published by the Editors of "Fortune," a high quality and authoritative magazine, clears up to a large degree the perplexing question of why wars in this supposedly civilized world are fought and prolonged.   The following is the gist of a chapter in the book entited, "Love Thine Enemy."   Read and weep—or get fighting mad, just as you feel inclined—but in any case be sure to squelch the inevitable urge to take down the old muzzle-loader, because the blunderbuss might blow up in your face.

The Editors of Fortune, by stating specific cases, prove that the Armorers, who are the true internationalists, regardless of their nationalities, work in unison with but two objectives—1st: *To prolong wars;* 2nd; *To disturb peace.* They further show that between 1814 and 1914 the internationalists worked assiduously and successfully at the unholy business of prolonging war.

Their method, the booklet states, was simple but most effective. It was this: if the enemy is running short of essentials with which to destroy your country's fighting men sell him what he needs out of your own supply.   The glorious carnage must not be hampered by nonsensical national loyalties.

So when Germany required glycerine to make high explosives with which to blow English, French and American boys to bits—or nickel, or copper, or oil, or rubber—English and French industries hastened to oblige by shipping these things to the enemy through Norway, Denmark, Switzerland, Spain and Holland. The internationalists of Germany graciously reciprocated by sending back through the same process of transshipment—enemy to neutral to enemy—things required by the enemy to blast German soldiers—iron, steel and essential engine parts.

The Editors of Fortune are very specific and state the authoritative sources of their startling information, as well as the amount of materials obligingly exchanged between the warring nations and when the transfers were made.

They then proceed to relate an spisode which, if positive proof had not accompanied the story, few would have believed that such a thing could be possible, if the eyes of the reader had not already been opened to behold the internationalist in his true light. They tell us about Briey and Dombasle.

The Briey basin, which supplied 70 per cent of the ore used by France, and where her great smelters and munition workers were located, passed unscathed into German hands quite early in the war. Then France advanced her lines once more and Briey was returned to her. German forces soon pushed the French lines back again and Briey was back in the German fold to pour out its tide of potential destruction and death.

But all during the conflict no shells from the big guns, nor bombs from airplanes, burst in the Briey basin. It was holy ground, sacred to the internationalists. When an American officer wanted to bomb the arsenal out of existence, and destroy the source of the suffering and death of his gallant troops, he was forbidden to do so. When he asked, *"Why"* he was given the following fiendish reply: *"If we shell Briey the Germans will, in reprisal, shell Dombasle."*

The Officer was dumbfounded. He had expected to have been told that the Allies intended to retake the Briey basin and desired to possess it intact, which might have allayed his wrath. But not so. It is stated that had Briey and Dombasle, from whence the metals and munitions for the most part unceasingly flowed, been destroyed when opportunity permitted, shortly after the World War began, the war would have ended in 1915. But the avaricious internationalists who owned the sources of supply got the warring enemies to agree not to shell the munitions works of each other— more especially the major ones at Briey and Dombasle. Thus the "Glorious War" went on and on—at a profit.

Please remember that only an armistice, not peace, was declared in 1918. World War II was fought over two opposing systems of economy; two distinct kinds of money. One kind is based on debt, the other on goods and services. Therefore the internationalists have no common ground on which to fraternize. The interest boys are out to destroy munition factories and all else which pays them no profits, and vice versa.

Now what do you think about the cry of a banker-subsidized press and war mongers in toto, by which the blood pressure of our brave fighting men was raised to the point of combat that they would willingly go across the seas— shed their blood—and in anguish, away from home and loved ones—*Die*—*"For the Preservation of Democracy"?*

"What fools we mortals be!"

What We Use for Money

Well, anyway, the bankers of America knew, in 1913, that a war of majestic proportions was about to begin— therefore, in order to be in a position to take the greatest possible advantage of the occasion, they decided to organize for the event. J. P. Morgan, the magnificent manipulator of the Rothschild's billions in America; Kuhn-Loeb, bankers, who donated $50,000,000 to finance the Red Revolution in Russia; and other Internationalists plunged merrily into the business of loaning money to the nations of Europe—vast sums of money. They knew that their investments were safe, although the nations to whom they loaned the money might be wiped out. They knew that by the use of a patriotically framed "war cry"—such as "A war to end all wars"—or, "A war for the preservation of Democracy"—this Nation could be incited to participate in the carnage, raise an army and go to Europe *to fight for the preservation of the bankers' loans.*

They knew further—that their hirelings in Congress could be depended upon and that the Government would, if the European warring nations became unable to repay the loans, raise the money and make good the losses of the International Bankers on their foreign loans. This was, of course, done—in its proper sequence—to the tune of several billion dollars, Mr. Morgan and his pals serenely stepping out of the picture and the people bearing the loss, with interest.

But to properly facilitate the exploitation of the people, the Federal Reserve Banking System was established in 1913. The Federal Reserve System was—and is—a *private banking institution.* It is not owned or controlled by the Government, as most people, because of its name, believe. The Government, through the Federal Reserve Board is granted supervisorial powers over it, but the Federal Reserve Board is comprised, in the main, of Governors of the Federal Reserve System—and *how awfully strict has their supervision of themselves turned out to be!!*

When a great California banker was asked by Andræ Nordskog, the author of "We Bankers," how it came about that the Secretary of the Treasury was no longer on the Federal Reserve Board, his reply was: "Because *we* kicked him off the board." Mr. Nordskog then asked why the President of the United States was no longer on the Board and his reply was: "Because *we kicked him off the board.*"

Do you remember Amschel Rothschild's boast—"Let me issue and control a nation's money and I care not who writes its laws"?

The United States Government does not own a single share of stock of the Federal Reserve System. All of the profits of the System were to have been turned over to the Government—but the Government has not received one cent of the System's profits.

The following illuminating statement was made in a report of the Federal Reserve System in 1918: "In its previous reports the Board has called attention to the fact that the Federal Reserve Banks are not operated primarily for profit, and it seems proper to reiterate this statement at this time, although it may seem incongruous in view of the fact that the combined gross earnings of the twelve banks for the year 1918 amounted to $67,584,117.00—the net earnings being $55,446,979.00."

1918 was probably an average year.

Starting from scratch in 1914, the Federal Reserve System began operations without a penny. Member banks, however, bought Federal Reserve Capital Stock in the amount of $134,000,000. That $134,000,000 produced profits in twenty-three years to a grand total, according to the Congressional Record of May 29, 1939, Page 8896, of $23,141,456,197. Not bad, eh!

In 1922 the consciences of the four bankers who are appointed by the President to operate the bank, at a salary of $15,000 annually, it appears, began to trouble them. In that year they got an amendment through Congress to the effect that the profits need no longer be paid to the Government, but would go into the reserves of the Bank. So now they do not steal the profits—they just take them.

The Federal Reserve System was designed to forever end bank failures in America. At least, such were the claims of the proponents of the bill. The noble objective was to be accomplished by the establishment of twelve Regional Federal Reserve Banks in as many districts, into which the Nation had been divided. When a money shortage loomed in one Regional District, on account of heavy seasonal demands, sufficient money was to have been transferred from the other Regional Banks to the Bank in that Region to provide ample funds to successfully transact all business demands.

In spite of this altruistic principle, which failed to materialize into fact, more banks have failed under the Federal Reserve System than at any other period in the history of the Nation—or of the world. In three years more than 14,000 banks closed their doors with multiplied billions of dollars of the people's hard earned money behind them.

The Federal Reserve System—which abhors Unions—is the most powerful, the most unscrupulous and the most un-Constitutional Union within the boundaries of the Nation. By maintaining the most powerful and most expensive lobby in Washinton, it dominates our Government—and through its far-reaching privileges it controls the life of every person living in the Nation. It makes of us all its interest paying bondsmen—and a *bondsman is a slave.* Let us see how this is accomplished.

Please bear in mind the fact that Article 1, Section 8, Paragraph 5 of the Constitution provides that the People of the Nation, through their elected Representatives, shall create the money of the Nation. The Constitution has, however, been set aside through the intrigue and power of the Bankers, and they—the Bankers—are now the money creators.

A comparatively paltry $3,292,245,392 is all the Constitutionally created money there is in the Nation. It is made up of the following: $346,681,016 of United States notes—or, as they were in derision dubbed, Lincoln Greenbacks. They were made in the Nation's Bureau of Printing and Engraving and were issued, interest free, to prosecute the Civil War when the Banks refused to loan Congress money at a lesser rate of interest than 28%. This amount is still outstanding—$103,318,984 of the $450,000,000 issued having been withdrawn from circulation and destroyed.

This small amount of *honest money* has saved the Nation more than $11,000,000,000 in interest. Issued Constitutionally—on the credit of the Nation—without the expensive formality of being backed by Government bonds, they provide us an example of the manner in which all of the Nation's money should be issued. However, to even the score, millions of dollars' worth of Civil War Bonds are still outstanding and still draw interest to the Banks.

In addition to the "Lincoln Greenbacks" we had, on August 30, 1940, $1,818,054,531 in Silver Certificates, issued, in part, Constitutionally, before silver was demonetized by the "Crime of 1873." These Silver certificates are supposed to have 100 cents in silver behind every dollar bill—but actually there is about 37 cents. I have already told you of the bitter fight of the Bankers against both of the above mentioned kinds of money, because, of course, this money paid the Bankers no interest—until after it was deposited in the Banks and loaned out, with many times— frequently up to thirty times—as much check-book money, from which time on it pays interest to the Bankers, *and how!*

We have, as a third classification, $1,129,346,723, in coin of various denominations, which is used for change. These three classifications of money comprise all of the honestly created, Constitutional money, there is in the Nation—with the exception of $1,163,122 in Treasury Notes of 1890 issue. This makes a grand total of $3,295,245,392 issued Contitutionally and outstanding—but not necessarily circulating—according to the United States Treasury Report of April 30, 1940.

In addition to this lawful money, there is $5,444,267,253 of unlawful money in the form of Federal Reserve Notes, Federal Reserve Bank Notes, and National Bank Notes, supposedly in circulation. This money is "unlawful money" as the face of the bills declares by stating that they will be redeemed in *"lawful money"* on demand.

If anyone but the special-privileged money creators and manipulators attempted to pass unlawful money, they would speedily go to prison for a long, long time—but our Government goes so far as to become a party to the act of counterfeiting.   To make this unlawful money legal, Congress, in 1935, at the behest of the President, declared all Federal Reserve Notes to be legal tender, thereby giving them the semblance of respectability.   They now bear on their face the stamp of the United States Government, which is intended to cover their depraved nature.   There is, then, at this time (April 1940) slightly more than $8,000,000 of circulating medium in the Nation. The difference between the amount of honestly created money and this figure is made up of these Federal Reserve Notes.   These notes are backed by Government bonds and are created in the following manner.

The Government needs, we will say $1,000,000000 for its Works Program.   Bonds for that amount are printed in the Bureau of Printing and Engraving, and as soon as—or even before, they are issued—the Federal Reserve Bank, by extending credit to the Government in the amount of the bond issue, buys the bonds.   The bonds are carted over to the Federal Reserve vaults, which gives the Government the right to draw checks against the Bank for the amount of the bonds.

The Bank, of course, draws interest from the Government (the People) on the billion dollars from the day the bonds are delivered.   Then, when the Bank needs new, or more currency, to transact its business, it takes the bonds over to the United States Treasury for safe-keeping and asks the Treasury Department for a billion dollars of new currency. The Bank is accommodated on condition that it will pay the printing bill. It is understood that it need not relinquish the bonds which it holds, but will continue to collect interest on them. The cost of printing new currency is, on the average, depending on the denomination of the notes demanded, $0.27 per thousand dollars, but, for convenience, we will say $0.30. Thus, we see, the Federal Reserve Bank obtains $1,000,000,000 of brand new money for $300,000. The Bank then loans the currency into circulation to anyone who can provide them with satisfactory collateral. *In fact each dollar of that $1,000,000,000 will be loaned to about thirty different people at the same time.*

By doing a little figuring one makes the astounding discovery that the gentlemen who shout the loudest, *"You can't get something for nothing,"* actually get theirs for less than thirty cents per thousand dollars and rake in interest on their investment at the rate of 9,583%. But even thirty cents per thousand is more than the Banks like to pay, so they manufacture about 95% of the Nation's purchasing power in their own laboratories, i.e.: their bank ledgers. More about that shortly.

While we are on the subject of Government bonds, let us consider them a little further. The questions which present themselves in this regard is— *"Why Government Bonds?"* —"Why $50,000,000,000 of them?"—"Why should bonds be issued as a basis of currency?"—"Why should the Government not print the money and *put directly into circulation in payment of its projects,* buildings, wars, warships and all other Governmental expenditures?"

Does the Banker's King Midas touch hallow, sanctify or increase the value of the Nation's money? You know as well as I that their mystic touch *decreases the value of the dollar.* Why does the newly created money have to go the round-about way of the Federal Reserve Bank? Why does it have to be put in the Bank—*with an equal amount of bonds—and then be borrowed out at high rates of interest?*

As an illustration, when Boulder Dam was built, at a cost of $160,000,000, *why should we have to pay $342,000,000 for it?*—Why should $182,000,000 more than the Dam cost go into the pockets of the Bankers? Why should we have to pay from 120% to 150% more for every mile of highway than the highway cost to construct? When a new Post Office is built in Los Angeles, at a cost of $7,000,000, why should we have to pay $16,000,000 for it—the Bankers getting the surplus?

When we foolishly enter a maniac's war across the seas and spend $26,000,000,000, like drunken sailors, why should we be saddled with bonds which will pay the Bankers $39,000,000,000 in interest? So on and on, far into the night—*or into a new day that has dawned.*

Please listen to *Thomas A. Edison,* for just a minute:

"People who will not turn a shovel full of dirt on the project (Muscle Shoals), nor contribute a pound of material, will collect more money from the United States than will the people who supply all the material and do all the work. *This is the terrible thing about interest.*

"In all great bond issues the interest is always greater than the principal. All the great public works cost more than twice as much on that account. Under the present system of doing business we simply add from 120% to 150% to the stated cost.

"But here is the point: *If the Nation can issue a dollar bond it can issue a dollar bill.* The element that makes the bond good makes the bill good also. The difference between the bond and the bill is that the bond lets the money broker collect twice the amount of the bond and an additional 20%. Whereas the currency, *the honest sort provided by the Constitution, pays nobody but those who contribute in some useful way.* It is absurd to say our country can issue bonds and cannot issue currency. Both are promises to pay, but one fattens the usurer and the other helps the people.

"If the currency issued by the people were no good, then the bonds would be no good either. It is a terrible situation when the Government, to insure the National wealth, must go in debt and submit to ruinous interest charges at the hands of men who control the fictitious value of gold.

"Interest is the invention of Satan."

Every baby, when born, faces an annual interest payment of $800 on account of our National debt. Every family in the nation owes, on an average, more than $2,000 a year, for the same reason—and our President stated, when opening the Congress, that the interest on our National debt is a first charge against the income of the Nation. A pair of shoes pays 156 different taxes and a loaf of bread 57 varieties. *If the banks were not more powerful than our Government we would have no national debt.* But even that phase of our money situation is not as serious a matter as that which I will now outline.

While there is $20,739,512,645 of lawful and unlawful United States money of all kinds in the world, there is approximately only about half that amount in circulation in the Nation—the other half being held in foreign capitals and in safety deposit boxes, tin cans and sugar bowls.

But here is the point: While there is less than $10,000,-000,000 of actual money on deposit in the Banks, there are total bank deposits of about $150,000,000,000. Well you may ask: "What then is deposited?" And the answer to that question is the answer to the greatest of all American tragedies.

The bank deposits of the Nation consist of the *homes,* the *farms,* the *vineyards,* the *orange groves,* the *factories,* the *stores,*—in brief, the real property and credit of the people of the Nation. Again you may ask: "How come?"

The answer is shocking, but it is true. It comes about by the Bankers making false ledger entries—namely: By entering a bank loan as a bank deposit. Let us illustrate: John Doe (who is typical of all) needs $1,000 in his business. He goes to the bank to arrange a loan. The Bankers ask him what collateral he can furnish and he is told that Mr. Doe has the deed to his home which he will turn over; or, he will give a mortgage on his farm—his chicken ranch —his business—or what have you.

The papers are arranged and John Doe hands over the collateral and signs a note which the Banker has prepared. If the collateral is not quite satisfactory, John is requested to get a co-signer or two—just in case. That done, the Banker calls a young fellow over to his desk and hands him a little slip of paper on which is the authorization for the boy to make an entry in the.bank ledger. When completed, the entry reads: "Bank Deposit—Joe Doe—$1,000.00."

Now, you see, John Doe hasn't deposited $1,000 at all. He has deposited his property. *The Banker has created* $1,000 *with the stroke of a pen* and has charged John Doe interest to the tune of $70 or $80 a year as remuneration for his magic trick. John Doe is provided with Bank Pass Book and a Check Book and is advised to sally forth and write checks against his Bank Account. Very little—about 5%—of the money ever leaves the Bank, so you see how it is that with $1,000,000 of money—which this Banker has obtained at a cost of $0.30 per thousand dollars—he is all set to prosecute his racket in a really big way. With $1,-000,000 of currency the Bank can make loans up to $30,-000,000—and claims to have on deposit the latter amount.

The Banker likes to think of this as *bank credit* but in reality it isn't bank credit at all. John Doe has supplied the credit but the Banker uses it and charges poor old John Doe for the privilege of turning it over to him and making it liquid. About 95% of the Nation's business is done with Banker-created fountain-pen money, and the bank check is used as a medium of exchange—*money*—which Congress alone has authority to issue, to do this 95% of the Nation's business.

Irving Fisher, the great economist of Yale University, and the author of the books, "100% Money," and "Stamp Scrip," declares that $1 of money supports $30 of so-called bank credit, or check-book money, or fountain-pen money, or synthetic money—whichever you prefer to call it.

This is a well established fact. There is less than *two cents behind each dollar of bank deposits in America.* There is only one dollar in cash in the banks to pay on $70 of Bank deposits.

Compared with the money manipulating, pen-juggling, crooked bookkeeping, unsocially minded bankers, operating legally if not ethically under our present money system—the Goldsmiths of old were veritable pikers.

They have succeeded in inveigling *the President of the United States,* and *Congress,* to commandeer all of the Gold from the People of the Nation on *threat of imprisonment*— and have had given to them either clear title to it or a first mortgage, in the form of *gold certificates,* on it (or at least 8/10ths of it), and then have buried it in the ground so that their debt-money system would not be hampered by a gold standard policy.

Most certainly, with the gold of the Nation in the possession of the International Bankers, it would be most unwise for the people of the Nation to demand a return to the coinage of gold or to a currency based on gold.

And currency should—and must be—issued debt and interest free, by Congress, against the wealth—the assets— the income—the production of the Nation—for on all of these is the taxing power of the Nation based.

When this is done, Banker exploitation and domination will be a thing of the past in America. This policy was in the minds of the Founding Fathers, who placed Article 1, Section 8, Part 5, in the Constitution which they wrote.

As a result of the present un-Constitutional and unethical way of doing business, eight-ninths of the Nation's wealth is already in hock to the bankers. We have a computed wealth of $280,000,000,000 in the Nation. There are debts against that wealth of $250,000,000,000. *Only one-ninth of the Nation's wealth is free from debt—and the bankers are not yet satisfied. They want possession of the remaining one-ninth.* If that is too much for you to accept from me, probably you will believe the Bankers themselves. Read on:

The Banker's Manifest

"Capital must protect itself in every way, through combination and through legislation. Debts must be collected and loans and mortgages foreclosed as soon as possible. When through a process of law *the common people have lost their homes, they will be more tractable and more easily governed by the strong arm of the law, applied by the central power of wealth, under control of leading financiers. People without homes will not quarrel with their leaders.* This is well known among *our principal men now engaged in forming an imperialism of capital to govern the world.* By dividing the people we can get them to expand their energies in fighting over questions of no importance to us *except as teachers of the common herd.* Thus by discreet action we can secure for ourselves what has been generally planned and successfully accomplished."

The above was printed from the *banker's manifest,* for private circulation among leading bankers only, taken from the Civil Servants' Year Book, "The Organizer" of January, and the "New American" of February, 1934.

So now you know why there are periods, of short duration, when loans are comparatively easy to obtain; why the Bankers call: *"Come and get it."* They who can create money by making a bookkeeping entry with a fountain pen, can just as easily destroy the money which they have created. They who have created a period of "easy money" can with the same facility, create a money stringency.

They will tell you that they wish the Community, State and Nation to be prosperous for, they say, it is during periods of prosperity that the Banks prosper. That is only a half truth—and a half truth is the most damnable of lies. It is true that during a prosperous period their money is more readily loaned at interest on satisfactory security, but it is *during the succeeding period of depression, when money is made tight, that the banker reaps his harvest by foreclosing on the real wealth of his mortgagors.* And the Bankers have an innate desire to *"go in and possess the land."* Remember the Bankers' statement above: *"This is well known among our principal men now engaged in forming an imperialism of capital to govern the world."*

It is very difficult for one who does not realize how devastatingly destrutive to all the finer human and spiritual instincts of man are the forces of avarice and greed, to believe that a group of supposedly Christian and non-Christian Americans, in whose hands is the power to first expand and then contract credit, with the object of gaining possession of the homes, farms, factories, etc., of their victims, to send them forth homeless and penniless to beg, steal, starve, take the pauper's oath, or commit suicide—but such are the grim facts of the case.

When the money-creating, interest-gathering, mortgage-holding Bankers go into their huddle and come up with the statement that there is a money shortage in the Nation and that loans must be called and mortgages foreclosed (if not paid) the Nation is about to be put, once again, through

the wringer and wrung dry. With only about 4,000,000,-
000 of actual money in circulation, they demand that loans
be paid—and "pronto." They know that it is a physical
impossibility for the mortgagors to pay off $69,000,000,-
000 of bank debts with only $4,000,000,000 of money—*for
your note or mortgage must be paid, not with bankers' fountain pen money but with legal tender.* The special privilege
to create money has been given by Congress to but a favored
few.

On an average of once every eleven years for a hundred
and fifty years, our accordion money system has been ex-
panded and collapsed—and with what tragic results. During the last seven years, so it has been stated, approximately
200,000 factory owners have lost their factories; 3,000,000
store keepers have lost their stores; more than 3,000,000
farmers have lost their farms—and *more than* 5,000,000
home owners have lost their homes through the process of
mortgage and foreclosure. An average of 600 families
every day for years, have been foreclosed upon and made
to give up their property to satisfy heartless greed in a land
which promises to all "Life, Liberty and the pursuit of
happiness."

A little of the tragic heart-break of those who are subjected to the ravages of our monetary system's greed may
be gathered from the incident here related.

Tomorrow Is Mother's Day

Yesterday there stood in Potter's Field, beside an open
grave, the forlorn figure of a weary man. His gray head
was bowed. His spare shoulders drooped as though they
bore a heavy load, and they shook, convulsed with grief.
Tears dripped from his hollow eyes upon the fresh-dug
earth of Potter's Field. It's hard to watch an old man weep.

Rough, careless hands quickly lowered a cheap coffin to
the bottom of the grave. Shovels were seized and then the

dreary sound of clods falling upon the lid of a wood box. The lonely man moved close, peered down through the rising dust into the yawning tomb and all the tenderness and love, all the desolate sadness, all the heart-broken agony of all the world was expressed by his wailing of a single word. That word was—"Mother."

No, she was not his mother who was being buried there, but his wife. But his term of endearment through the years for her had been "Mother" Ever since their sons were born, 40 years ago, he had called her "Mother." The two fine boys were the idols of their mother's heart, and the pride of their father's life. But they had heard what they thought to be the call to what they mistook for duty and had been killed in battle on distant, foreign soil. When the word arrived of the death of the first, and then within a month, the second son, the very earth seemed to reel and rock and the foundations of the universe to dissolve beneath the parents' feet. Nothing mattered now.

The mother moved about as in a trance and the stunned father could scarcely pull himself together. Finally he was told that he was too old to do the work required of him (he was then 46), and a younger man took his place. For awhile he worked at any odd job he could find, but soon there were none of those.

One day they received notice that the payment on the mortgage on their home was over-due and must be paid at once. Futilely the man tried to find work to earn the necessary money, but he was 47 now, and who would employ a man of that advanced age. He saw the banker and reminded him that he had paid $3,000 on the $1,500 mortgage—$1,800 going for interest, $1,200 to reduce the principal and that now, after 22 years only $300 remained unpaid. He begged for leniency. An extension of three months was granted but they proved to be months of frustration and terrible foreboding.

The appointed day arrived and with it a notice from the bank to vacate within two weeks or they would be forcibly evicted. The little mother's crushed heart was in her home. She had been brought to it as a bride. Her boys had been born there. Millions of sweet memories clung to its every board and sash and sill. The trees, the birds, the shrubs, the flowers and the smooth lawn were all intimate friends. The old home had a sentimental value of a million dollars and now it must be lost for a paltry $300.

And what new horrors did the future hold? The awful uncertainty. Where could they go? What could they do? They had no money to rent another place nor to move elsewhere. Baffled, stunned, defeated, all they could do, it seemed, was wait and pray that the heart of the banker would soften.

The fatal day arrived and with it an order to vacate and men to see that the order was obeyed. Ruthlessly the furniture, pictures, knick-knacks, clothing and all were piled in a jumbled heap on the lawn. The little mother was helped to a chair beneath the palm tree she had planted the spring her first baby was born. Her husband gently stroked her hair and placed a protecting arm about her shoulders—small protection indeed against the hosts of entrenched greed.

A decision was made. Their belongings must be sold to supply their present need. A second hand dealer was called and upon arriving arrogantly asked: "Well, what do you want for this pile of junk?"

A pitifully few dollars bought those objects which were more precious than gold to those who had sacrificed through the long years to accumulate them. The lawn was soon cleared and arm in arm the two, in silence, trudged slowly down the familiar street as the sun sank behind the Western hills.

Twenty years have passed since that man and his wife were dispossessed. For twenty years he did his best to earn an honest living and for twenty years she lived in rooms, cubby-holes, garrets, or wherever they could find shelter. She had worked, too, as she could—scrubbing, sewing, washing, nursing—but always with an aching heart. Recently at 58 years of age, she dropped the load and died. Yesterday she was given Christian burial in Potter's Field. The old man will stagger on—alone. *Tomorrow is Mother's Day.*

Pauperization Through Interest

It is surely quite obvious that a money system based on debt will ultimately ruin any nation and every person in the nation except the money lender. One cent loaned at 6% compound interest the day Christ was born would now amount to the tidy sum of $95,965,240,000,000,000,000,-000,000,000,000,000,000,000,000,000. If this amount were in gold and rolled into a ball, the ball would be larger than the earth.

If one of your ancestors had possessed sufficient foresight to invest just $1 for you, 500 years ago, at 6% compound interest, you would now be heir to $1,078,631,139,556. The total net income of the United States for the past 17 years would not match your income through your ancestor's investment of a single dollar.

Andræ Nordskog, in his splendid book, "We Bankers," relates a rather startling incident which illustrates for us the fact that we cannot keep on going in the direction in which we are headed, without meeting disaster. He states as follows:

"In February, 1850, our State of California issued bonds in the sum of $934.40 to pay for a granite slab to be placed at the 120 foot level inside of Washington's Monument on the grounds of our National Capitol.

"On the slab is the following inscription: 'California,

Youngest of the Union, Brings Her Golden Tribute to the Memory of Its Father.'

"Our Golden State issued short term bonds bearing interest at the rate of 36% annually. In 1873 new bonds, in the amount of $2,277,500.00 were issued to retire the original bonds. Since that time *the State has paid over* $10,000,000 in interest but not one cent on the principal."

For whom is democracy working?

If all of the debts in the nation were paid there would not be a single dollar in circulation in the nation. Rather a startling statement, isn't it? Yet it is Gospel truth. The only way to get money into circulation is for somebody to borrow, on mortgages, notes, bonds, or other securities, from the banks—*so the banks collect interest on every dollar, whether it be constitutional money, Federal Reserve Notes or banker-created check-book money.* Our annual interest bill on our public and private debts amounts to almost $15,000,000,000 (1941).

Since the people have either lost the heart to borrow from the Banks, or their collateral has already been taken over by the Banks—the latter being primarily the case—and therefore can no longer borrow, *in order to get money into circulation the Government must do the borrowing* in lieu of the people. That is the reason for the recent borrowing —"Lending-Spending Program."

Just how much farther the Nation can get into debt to the Banks and maintain a semblance of power, is a moot question. Probably another war, with its resultant bond issue—or the present defense program—will turn the trick. Another $25,000,000,000 of Government Bonds in the hands of the International Bankers, added to the $50,000,-000,000 which they now hold, will probably supply the excuse for them to move in and say to the President and Congress: *"Gentlemen, in order to secure our investment we must take over the Government!!"*

The following statements were made by men who viewed with apprehension the situation in our Nation:

Woodrow Wilson

"A great industrial Nation is controlled by its system of credit. Our system of credit is concentrated. The growth of the Nation and all our activities are in the hands of a few men. We have come to be one of the worst ruled, *one of the most. completely controlled and dominated* Governments in the world—no longer a Government of free opinion, no longer a Government by conviction *and vote of the majority, but a Government by the opinion and duress of small groups of dominant men."*

Honorable Charles A. Lindbergh

"Under the Federal Reserve Act *panics are scientifically created:* the present (1920) is the first scientifically created one, worked out as we figure a mathematical problem."

Frank A. Vanderlip, 1935

"We have already tried borrowing and spending our way to recovery, we have had numberless hopeful and well-meant experiments, aimed to bring us out of the depression. Thus far we have not emerged, *nor will until the fatal defects of our money system are corrected.* To those defects, more than anything else, I attribute the depression."

Marriner Eccles

(Chairman Federal Reserve System, 1935)
"The banks can create and destroy money. Bank credit money. It is the money we do most of our business with, not with that currency which we usually think of as money."

Robert H. Hemphil

(Credit Manager Federal Reserve Bank in Atlanta)
"If all the bank loans were paid no one would have a bank deposit and *there would not be a dollar of coin or currency in circulation.* This is a staggering thought. *We are completely dependent on the commercial banks. Someone has to borrow every dollar we have in circulation, cash or credit. If the banks create ample synthetic money we are prosperous; if not, we starve.* We are absolutely without a permanent money system. When one gets a complete grasp of the picture *the tragic absurdity of our hopeless position is almost incredible,* but there it is. It [the banking problem] is the most important subject intelligent persons can investigate and reflect upon. *It is so important that our present civilization may collapse unless it becomes widely understood and the defects remedied very soon."*

Irving Fisher

(Professor Emeritus Economics at Yale)
"When a bank lends or invests, it extends credit, i.e., creates check-book money. When it gets loans paid, or sells investments, it contracts credit, i.e., destroys check-book money. In normal times such creation and destruction of money roughly balance. *But when they do not balance, the Nation's money is inflated and deflated and causes a boom or a depression."*

Sumner H. Slichter

(Professor Business Economics at Harvard)
"When banks grant credit by creating or adding to bank deposits, subject to check, *new dollars* are *created.* It is true that the new dollars are not stamped out of gold. They are credit dollars and are *created by the stroke of a pen* rather

than by dies and stamping machines, but their purchasing power is not less than the dollars coined at the Government Mint.

"In other words, the principal way in which dollars are created is by borrowing. This means that the number of dollars in existence at any particular time *depends upon the ability and willingness of the banks to lend.* The volume of purchasing power fluctuates with the state of men's minds; *the growth of pessimism may suddenly throw millions of men out of work, or the growth of confidence may create thousands of jobs overnight."*

Abraham Lincoln

"Government possessing power to create and issue currency and credit as money and enjoying the right to withdraw currency and credit from circulation by taxation and otherwise, *need not and should not borrow capital at interest,* as the means of financing Governmental work and public enterprise. *The Government should create, issue and circulate all currency and credit needed to satisfy the spending power of the Government and the buying power of consumers. The privilege of creating and issuing money is not only the supreme prerogative of Government, but it is the Government's greatest creative opportunity."*

Abraham Lincoln
(Just before his assassination)

"I see in the near future a crisis approaching that unnerves me and causes me to tremble for the safety of my country: corporations have been enthroned, an era of corruption in high places will follow, and the money power of the country will endeavor to prolong its reign by working upon the prejudices of the people until the wealth is aggregated in a few hands, and the Republic is destroyed."

Franklin D. Roosevelt

"Sixty families in America control the wealth of the Nation."

"One-third of the Nation's Population is ill-housed, ill-fed and ill-clad."

"Twenty per cent of the men working on W. P. A. projects are in such an advanced state of malnutrition that they cannot do a day's work."

"I intend to drive the money changers from the temple."

National Research Committee

From a recent report of a Committee composed of twenty-five economists, engaged by Congress to make a National survey:

"Purchasing power must be gotten into the hands of the people if Democracy is to survive."

CHAPTER IX

Money System Based on Debt Fails

Our money system, based on debt, has been in operation for 196 years (1764-1960). One hundred ninety-six years of trial should be a sufficiently long period of time in which to prove any system. Weighed in the balance of the years the *Nation's money system is found wanting.* Abraham Lincoln's prophecy is all but fulfilled. The Nation's wealth is now possessed by a few men and the Republic is well nigh destroyed.

President Roosevelt told us that 60 families in America are in control of the wealth of the Nation. Amschel Rothschild said:—"Let me issue and control a nation's money and *I care not who writes its laws."* Those who are in control of the money are more mighty than all our lawmakers and legislators combined. Less than 1% of the people have been influencing our thinking and controlling our voting. It is well that the people have become awakened in the nick of time—*or is it in the nick of time?—or have we become awakened?*

The history of nations proves that when 10% of the people control 90% of the wealth, the nation is doomed. *We are just about there!*

Eight-ninths of the Nation's wealth is already in the hands of the Bankers. And they want to gain possession of the remaining one-ninth. Our annual interest bill is nearly $15,000,000,000; our crime bill is about the same— and dividends to corporation heads on *watered stock* fully as much.

In 1936, those who do the work of the nation—39,450,-

300 persons—received for their labor $25,862,800,000, an average of $658.80 each.   Forty-six per cent of these—or 18,358,954 persons—received an average income of $588 each—while one-tenth of one per cent, 5,387 persons, had an average income of $203,368.   One person in the higher strata received as much as 346 persons in the lower strata.

Probably the thought may present itself that those in the lower strata are on "Relief," and shouldn't count.   It is true a part of them are on "Relief"—but just why they are, is another story; and, after all, this Nation is founded upon the principle "That all men are created equal."   Most certainly all have an equal claim to *"Life, liberty, and the pursuit of happiness."*

But we will step up one stratum from the bottom and step down one from the top—and see what we shall see. We find in the next group 13,920,349 employed persons received an average of $1,406—while there were 13,341 in the second group from the top who received an average of $69,664 each.   One person in the higher strata received as much for swinging a fountain pen and a golf club as 50 in the lower strata earned swinging a hammer or operating a machine.

The famous *Brookings Institute* made a national survey and found that the average income of the workers of the Nation is only $740 per year, while the amount required to live on—according to American standards—is $1,550.   Research authorities and economists tell us that there is sufficient wealth in America for every person to have an annual income of $4,700.

Because of the lack of purchasing power in the hands of the vast majority of the people, the consuming power of the Nation is at a mighty low ebb.   If money did not have to be borrowed from the Bankers to find its way into circulation, but were issued by the Nation against its producing ability and consuming capacity, whereby profits would be made out of the sale of produce and manufactured goods instead of interest charges on the Nation's purchasing power, there would be no unemployment and no business stagnation in America. Article 1, Section 8, Paragraph 5 of the Constitution of the United States very wisely provides for just that kind of a money system. *What's holding us back?*

Lack of money in the hands of the potential customers stops the retailer from selling; if he doesn't sell to the customer he doesn't buy from the wholesaler; and if he doesn't buy from the wholesaler, the wholesaler doesn't buy from the distributor; and if the wholesaler doesn't buy from the distributor, the distributor doesn't buy from the manufacturer; and if the distributor doesn't buy from the manufacturer the manufacturer doesn't buy from the miller, the miner, the farmer, the rancher—and thus production is killed at its source, all because the consumer lacks purchasin power, and the reason he lacks it is *directly traceable to a dishonest money system.*

They will tell you that the thing that will pull us out of the "Depression" is *Industry.* Get the factories running and they will use the goods produced by the producers of raw materials, thus putting men to work producing more goods. The factories will employ more men in the manufacture of goods and they will begin to buy so that the wholesalers will have to begin to stock up to supply the merchants. So our Government prints up some bonds and borrows money from the Federal Reserve Bank—(credit money, of course, just as though the Bank's credit were better than that of the Nation; whereas, it is after all the Nation's credit which the Bank uses and charges the Nation interest on)—and loans it to the factory owner, hoping that a little of it will trickle down to the consumer so that goods may be bought.

Any school boy knows that the roots of the tree—not the

branches—need the irrigation. If water is poured freely on the roots the fruit will soon appear on the branches. Why not pour the water of much needed purchasing power on the roots of our withered industrial and commercial tree? Why keep on sprinkling the branches. Why not supply the consumers of the Nation with consuming power and break the log jam in our River of Business so that from the mouth of the river right back to its source it will flow, an unimpeded stream?

There is another reason why we must change from the present way of doing things. We will have to face the fact that we are living in a new age—an age in which the mighty giant water-fall has been harnessed to perform the work of puny man,—an age when one-eighth of a cent's worth of electrical energy, applied to a modern machine, can do the work of a man working an eight-hour day at a cost of from $4 to $12—an age in which a gallon of gasoline exploded in an internal combustion engine produces energy equal to one hundred man-hours of toil.

We are living in a day when the brain of man is superseding the brawn of man and the curse pronounced upon man—"In the sweat of thy face shalt thou eat bread"—has been removed. The Light of the World, "Who lighteneth every man that cometh into the world," who came to redeem men from "The Curse of a Broken Law," has illuminated the minds of men, causing inventions to spring forth so that "All who labor and are heavy laden" have, through their inspired ingenuity, found rest.

Earth-digging, road-building, mountain-moving, soil-turning, coal-mining, rock-crushing, cement-mixing, brick-laying, goods-hauling, lumber-sawing, grain-harvesting, cotton-picking, steel-rolling linotype-setting, tree-felling, land-plowing, cloth-making, steel-pressing, sand-blasting, glass-blowing, figure-calculating, typewriter-operating, garment-cutting, box-making, parcel-wrapping, fruit-canning, potato-digging, corn-planting, cotton-chopping, vine-spraying, garden-cultivating, grass-mowing, vacuum-cleaning, cable-laying, auto-painting, car-washing—ad infinitum machines have been devised and put into general use with the inevitable result, the *disemployment of millions of workmen:* workmen who will never return to their wage-earning labor.

By the use of the modernized machinery which we now have in operation, four hours of work per day, four days per week, by the workers of the Nation, would produce all that the Nation, at the present rate of consumption, would consume. Still other machines are perfected, which, if put into use, would greatly increase production at still lower cost with a still greater decrease of necessary man power.

The complete mechanization of industry is the objective of the industrialist. A man-less factory is his dream—a factory in which the machines are set in motion and operated by an electrical engineer in a control room. Some such factories are a practical reality. The American trend is toward the disemployment of every man possible. Industry has developed a "Frankenstein" monster which will destroy its ingenious creator, for disemployed men are transformed from a national asset into a national liability through lack of ability to consume the products of the factory which has disemployed them. Men becoming disemployed must be provided with adequate purchasing power to live according to "American Standards" if "American Standards" are to be maintained.

Furthermore, the way to preserve Americanism is to provide for the maintenance of American standards of living. No foreign "ism" on earth could gain headway in America if the submerged third of the Nation's population shared in the abundance which abounds on every hand. Discontent is the result of economic and industrial shortsightedness.

What is to become of the men who are now disemployed

—and the still greater number who will become disemployed through technological advancement?

One-third of our population is now dependent on Charity or "Relief" for their very existence—"and the end is not yet." Those who lack social consciousness have said: *"When an animal in the jungle gets too old to fight for its own existence it is left to die. When an Eskimo becomes too old or infirm to keep up with the rest he is sealed in an igloo and permitted to die."* They would apply the policy of the jungle to an economy which they control.

Civilization has created a society by which every member of that society either voluntarily conforms to the decrees of that society or is compelled so to do.

The society which sets up moral and legal limitations for the control of the conduct of those comprising that society, is responsible to the members of that society, so long as its rules are enforced.   As another has aptly said: *"A society which says, 'Work or starve'—and then fails to provide work* (or its equivalent), *"is failing in its duties and responsibilities to the members of that society."*

Because of the disemployment of 12,000,000 workers by an unconstitutional money system and the mechanization of the Nation, that number of persons [mostly heads of families,] have been deprived of their power to consume through lack of purchasing power.   They still possess the desire to consume but their desires are incapable of fulfillment.   *The machines which have displaced the men do not consume,* therefore we have the paradoxical condition of *starvation in the midst of abundance.*

The cotton planting, cultivating, chopping and picking machines have disemployed millions of men, but the machines do not wear overalls or shirts, while the men who have been disemployed by the machine cannot buy them— so every third row of cotton (or thereabouts) must be plowed under, while acres of bales of unsold cotton are still on hand. *The fact of the matter is, if all those who work in cotton had a mattress to sleep on there would be no over-production of cotton in America.*

Modernized farm machinery has disemployed millions of farm laborers. The machines do not eat bread and the disemployed laborers, for lack of purchasing power, can't—so farmers are paid for not growing wheat. An extra slice of bread a day in the stomachs of the one-third who are ill-fed, would solve our "over-production of wheat" problem.

While children are growing into weaklings, because of malnutrition (and who will, according to a leading authority, be unfit for war in case of invasion) which will seriously affect the future of the Nation; and while children are unable to study in school because of rickets and weakness through lack of vitamins—*orange dumps a mile long, where millions of boxes of choice oranges are sprayed with creosote to make them unfit for human consumption, have been seen and photographd in California, to artificially boost prices.*

If the Associated Farmers (who are, in reality, the *Associated Bankers*—or are completely dominated by them) *did not hold a dollar in higher esteem than a human life,* oranges could be made available to all. Why not provide orange bins on school grounds where children could help themselves? The oranges, instead of being destroyed, could very easily be hauled, at a small cost to any school district—and how much more restful should be the sleep of the rascals who now destroy them. One orange grower did haul a truck load of oranges to the school in his district. The next day he was visited by an official of the Associated Farmers (or Orange Growers) and was told that if he gave any more oranges away the *association would not buy another one of his oranges.*

In 1938, one-third of the melon crop in the Imperial Valley was destroyed in order to insure sufficiently high prices for that which was marketed to warrant producers raising melons the next year. While this was going on the All American Canal was being completed, at a cost of about $100,000,000 of money borrowed from the Bankers, for the use of which the Government will pay fully $120,000,-000 in interest.

Mr. Harold Ickes stated, when opening the canal, that the water from it would double the acreage planted to melons. *Can you beat it?*

In the San Joaquin Valley, 500,000 tons of grapes were reported destroyed in 1938 and thousands of tons of Sun Maid Raisins were saturated with fish oil to make them inedible, while at the same time a Dam is in course of construction across the San Joaquin River at a cost of about $50,000,000 of money borrowed from the Bankers, to irrigate more of the San Joaquin Valley, so that more land may be brought under cultivation for the growing of grapes —so that more grapes can be destroyed.

Six million cases of canned peaches were carried over from the 1937 pack, making it unnecessary to can any peaches raised in the Sacramento Valley in 1938. Some of the choicest ones were canned but not because the market demanded them. One could wade through peaches half way to the knees and the stench of decaying fruit almost drove one out of the County. Other foodstuffs and fruits were also left to rot on the ground.

What is being done to remedy that situation? Why, the Government has borrowed over $60,000,000 from the Bankers to build a dam at Shasta across the Sacramento Valley in order that more peaches may be grown to be destroyed or left to rot.

While farmers are being paid for not growing wheat, the greatest water project in the world is being constructed at a cost of more than $170,000,000 of Banker borrowed money at Bonneville, across the Columbia River so that more Washington and Oregon wheat land will be brought under cultivation for the growing of wheat so that more farmers can be paid for not growing wheat.

It is said that when a person is taken to the insane asylum his condition is sometimes tested by being placed in a room where a water faucet is opened and water allowed to run over the floor. The person under test is given a mop and told to mop up the water. If he tries to mop up the water without turning the faucet off they know he is crazy. Not only is the faucet of production allowed to run, but it is opened still wider at the expense of the taxpayer, while the surplus overflow is being mopped up through the food destruction program. Are lunatics in charge of the American nut house?

Under our present economic system of borrow and spend, this asinine program seems to be necessary for the simple reason that the only way that money can be put into circulation is to borrow it, and since the people have lost either the will or the ability, through prior loss of their collateral, Congress must borrow in order that purchasing power may be in circulation—hence an ever increasing, and already enormous, National debt of $50,000,000,000*—the interest on which will amount to more than $70,000,000,000,- making a grand total, on the basis of our present debt, of $130,000,000,000.

Why Borrow Money?

Why should the money be borrowed, at high rates of interest, to construct these and hundreds of other great Government projects? *Why should Congress not obey the edict of Article 1, Section 8, Paragraph 5, of the Constitution,* and coin the money necessary for the construction of its

*This is for 1941. It is interesting to observe that the U. S. National Debt jumped to $275,000,000,000 in 1950 (see U. S. Dept. of Commerce, Statistical Abstract of the U. S., p. 360).

projects. When that is done, and the projects are function-
ing to increase the consumable goods of the Nation, what is
to prevent the Congress issuing purchasing power directly
to the people, through its retired senior citizens, thus solving the Nation's Relief and Unemployment problems without adding to the tax load of the Nation?

And now our Defense Program looms before us like a
mountain. Already the debt ceiling of the Nation has been
raised to permit still greater borrowing. It is quite apparent
that by the time the Nation has anything like adequate defense, to say nothing of what appears to be our inevitable
involvement in the war, the National debt will reach at least
$75,000,000,000. ($280,000,000,000 in 1959.)

As much as we may disapprove of Hitler, his regimenta-
tion and his ambitions, it must be recognized that he put
into effect a money system by which goods and services were
transferred without paying a toll to those "Who toiled not
—neither did they spin."

At this point a letter addressed to President Roosevelt
by Judge John Curtiss Hamm, of Temple City, California,
will be introduced to convey the point.

May 15, 1940

Honorable Franklin D. Roosevelt
President of the United States,
The White House,
Washington, D. C.
My dear Mr. President:

The little pieces of paper (marks) have done it.

While unrestricted issuance of paper money twenty years
ago caused inflation of currency and the collapse of the
German nation, restricted issue of paper money (requiring
a mark's worth of goods production or services rendered
for every mark issued) caused an inflation of production
exactly commensurate with the inflation of the currency, and

made the German nation one in purpose and great in power —great enough to very probably command the whole globe.

"We were not foolish enough to try to make a currency coverage of gold of which we had none, but for every mark that was issued we required an equivalent of a mark's worth of work done or goods produced."— Adolph Hitler.

Little pieces of paper made Germany in six years a nation whose power challenges the world because those little pieces of paper put people to work, gave them food, unified them into a phalanx behind their leaders, and builded an empire whose boundaries if they continue to extend will encompass the earth.

Why can't American statemanship take this lesson to heart? Why wait to raise money by taxation or issue more bonds before putting people to work?

There is on the books authority for issuing three billion dollars in currency. Why not issue it as Germany did, a dollar bill for a dollar's worth of actual production or labor and thus make a unified, contented, loyal people?

Of course it would not suit the coupon clipping bond-holders—the money changers in the temple. But is there not on record a promise that they were to be driven out? And are not the people awaiting for the fulfillment of that promise?

This is all that stands in the way of a unification and solidarity hitherto unknown in these United States.

I am an American.

Faithfully yours,
(Signed) JUDGE JOHN CURTIS HAMM
Temple City, California.

Debunking the Inflation Bugaboo

When the subject of Constitutional money is raised, the Bankers and their parrots cry *"Inflation"* from the house tops. They shout "Printing Press Money" and "Fiat Money," to scare their ignorant and uninformed dupes into submission.

Let us look at the matter squarely. What other kind of money than "printing press" money have we in America? All currency is printing press money. Its substitute is check-book money. Now which is better—for the Government to issue printing press money or to give the Bankers the privilege to issue check-book money?

As we have shown you, there is $69,000,000,000 of check-book money in circulation and on deposit. How would it cause "inflation" if instead, that were Constitutionally issued currency, which would mean that there would be 100 cents behind each dollar of bank deposits instead of one and two-thirds cents (1 2/3c.), as is now the case.

Fiat money is money issued by command of the State or Government. Well, isn't that the kind of money we want, and for which the Constitution makes provision?

The Bankers will say: "Just look what the over-issuance of money did to Germany during and after the World War."

Well—who did it? It was the Bankers, through the Reichbank, who did it. And they did it intentionally. It was done so that they and their "Pals" could pay their debts with inflated money, and thus get out from under at a fraction of a cent on the dollar. And, moreover, the inflated currency was not matched by goods and services in the nation.

No, my Friends, a scientific Board of Economists, appointed and supervised by Congress—which would be no longer dominated by the Bankers and which would, therefore, work in the interests of all of the people of the Nation —could issue and regulate the value of money a great deal more satisfactorily than a group of avaricious and unscientific Bankers.

What the Bankers mean when they cry *"Inflation"* is that they would no longer be in a position to first inflate and then deflate the Nation's purchasing power to their own advantage.

The way to end *"Deflation"*—which is a great deal more disastrous than "inflation"—as well as uncontrolled *"Inflation,"* is to take the power to create and control the money out of the hands of private Bankers and place it in the hands of men who are responsible to the people who elect and appoint them.

Don't let them scare you with their self-centered cries. They always shout for their own interests and not for yours —and of course the way they shout is through their Charley McCarthy, subsidized newspapers. Do the opposite to that which the major portion of the Metropolitan press advises and you will be working in your own and the people's interests.

An increase of purchasing power in the hands of those who now lack it is the crying need of the hour. That cannot be accomplished so long as we have a money system based on debt; and a money system based on debts is the only kind that the Bankers like. Their definition of sound money is money which pays them interest. Money which pays them no interest is, they say, unsound money. *Nonsense!!*

Why should 27 cents of every earned dollar go to the Bankers to make their money sound? Why should we pay the Bankers $15,000,000,000 yearly just to safeguard against *"Inflation"?*

There is a much less expensive way than that to do it. Place the power to create the money and to regulate its value in the hands of Congress, for which the Constitution provides—and then, if they cannot supply efficient money to transact the Nation's business at capacity production and consumption, *replace them with men who have sufficient stuff above their ears to do the job,* for most certainly *it can be and it must be done.*

Our Patriotic Statesmen

We have several patriotic statesmen among the many traitorous politicians in Washington, who take seriously their oath of office by which they swear to preserve and defend the Constitution of the United States and who remember that Article 1, Section 8, Part 5 is a part of that Constitution.   These are determined to restore the issuing power of money to Congress and to make of the Federal Reserve System the Governmental institution which it is believed by the vast majority of citizens to be.

These true Representatives of the people have prepared from time to time, Bills to remedy this basic National evil, but invariably they have failed to secure a sufficient number of signatures to bring their Bills out of Committee onto the floor of the House for discussion. Two hundred eighteen signatures are required, but only half that number of elected Representatives have been willing to disregard the Bankers' order and sign the petitions.

The Honorable H. Jerry Voorhis, representing the 12th Congressional District of California, had a Bill in Committee which would, if enacted, turn the trick. This Bill, in substance was as follows—and surely no patriot would refuse to sign it:

"BILL (H. R. 8209), by JERRY VOORHIS to PURCHASE FEDERAL RESERVE BANKS.

Be it enacted, etc., That (a) the Secretary of the Treasury of the United States is hereby authorized and directed to purchase the capital stock of the 12 Federal Reserve Banks and branches and agencies thereof, and pay to the owners thereof the par value of such stock at the time of purchase.

(b) All member banks of the Federal Reserve System are hereby required and directed, to deliver forthwith to the Treasurer of the United States by execution and delivery of such documents as may be prescribed by the Secretary of the Treasury, all of the stock of the said Federal Reserve Banks owned or controlled by them, together with all claims of any kind or nature in and to the capital stock of said Federal Reserve Banks, it being the intention of this Act to vest in the Government of the United States, the absolute, complete and unconditional ownership of the said Federal Reserve Banks."

There was also a Senate Resolution which had been introduced by Senator Lynn Frazier, and which struck at the very heart of the tragedy. It is Senate Joint Resolution No. 188, and read as follows:

"JOINT RESOLUTION

To restore to Congress the sole power to issue money and regulate the value thereof.

WHEREAS the national banks of the United States from and since 1863 have been operating contrary to the provisions of the Federal Constitution; and

WHEREAS the Federal Reserve System has, since 1913, been operating contrary to the provisions of the Federal Constitution, and that both of the aforesaid institutions have un-constitutionally used the power of Congress to issue and regulate the value of money contrary to the Constitution; and

WHEREAS the Constitutional provision has never been modifid, amended, or repealed; Therefore, be it

RESOLVED by the Senate and House of Representatives of

the United States of America in Congress assembled;
That said national banks and said Federal Reserve Board,
and the member banks of the Federal Reserve System,
be, and they are hereby, declared to be operating without
any Constitutional authority; and be it further

RESOLVED, That said institutions and each of them shall not,
after eighteen months from the passage of this resolution be permitted to issue any money or have any control
of the money and credit of the United States; and be it
further

RESOLVED, That if said institutions or either of them obtain
credit from the Government of the United States, it shall
be on the same terms and conditions as the credits extended by Government to other institutions and individuals; and be it further

RESOLVED, That a joint committee of both Houses of Congress be appointed to formulate a plan to be presented to
the Congress for the future regulation of money."

In 1933 Congress took the reassuring manifesto of President Roosevelt seriously, believing that he meant what he
said when he promised to "Drive the money changers from
the temple."

Congress put through a Bill in 1933, titled "Financing
and Exercising Power Conferred by Section 8 of Article 1,
of the Constitution: To Coin Money and to Regulate the
Value Thereof."

This Bill was intended to provide debt and interest free
Constitutionally issued money to be used in part to pay the
Soldiers' War Bonus—but it was not put into effect by the
President. It still stands on the Statute Books, an indisput-
able evidence of banker domination of the Nation's Gov-
ernment.

Copy of this Bill may be found on Page 151 of the Book
entitled "Federal Reserve Act of 1913, With Amendments

and Laws Relating to Banking," compiled by Elmer A. Lewis, Superintendent Document Room, House of Representatives, and states in part as follows:

"(b) If the Secretary, when directed by the President is unable to secure the assent of the several Federal Reserve Banks and the Federal Reserve Board to the agreements authorized in this (preceding) section or if operations under the above provisions prove to be inadequate to meet the purposes of this section, or if for any other reason additional measures are required in the judgment of the President to meet such purposes, then the President is authorized—

(1) To direct the Secretary of the Treasury to cause to be issued in such amount or amounts as he may from time to time order, United States Notes, as provided in the Act entitled 'An Act to authorize the issue of United States Notes and for the redemption of funding thereof and for funding the floating debt of the United States,' approved February 25, 1862, and Acts supplementary thereto and amendatory thereof, in the same size and of similar color to the Federal Reserve Notes heretofore issued and in denominations of $1, $5, $10, $20, $50, $100, $500, $1,000, and $10,000; but notes issued under this subsection shall be issued only for the purpose of meeting maturing Federal obligations to repay sums borrowed by the United States and for purchasing United States Bonds and other interest-bearing obligations of the United States: *Provided,* That when any such notes are used for such purpose the bond or other obligation so acquired or taken up shall be retired and cancelled. Such notes shall be issued at such times and in such amounts as the President may approve but the aggregate amount of such notes outstanding at any time shall not exceed $3,000,000,000. . . .

Instead of pursuing the Constitutional policy authorized

by Congress, the President chose to issue more bonds and to borrow more money from the bankers, for which our children's children will be paying interest.

The following is an excerpt from a letter written at the request of the President in reply to several telegrams sent to him by the Author. By it you will be able to judge whether or not President Roosevelt is sincere in his avowal to "Drive the Money Changers from the Temple," and whether or not he stands in defense of the Constitution of the United States:

May 31, 1940

Dear Mr. Elsom:

There has been referred to us from the White House your telegram inquiring about the issuance of debt and interest free Constitutional money.

By "debt-free' it is presumed that you mean unsecured currency and it would seem that the question you are asking is why the Federal Government does not issue unsecured currency to finance public expenditures instead of selling interest bearing securities.

The general objections to unsecured currency issues were well stated by the President in his message to Congress of May 22, 1935, disapproving the act of Congress for the immediate payment of adjusted service certificates (the Patman Bonus Bill). That message contained the following:

"The second 'whereas' clause, which states that the payment of certificates will not create an additional debt, raises a fundamental question of sound finance. To meet a claim of one group by this deceptively easy method of payment will raise similar demands for the payment of claims of other groups. It is easy to see the ultimate result of meeting recurring demands by the issuance of Treasury notes. It invites an ultimate reckoning in uncontrollable prices and in the destruction of the value of savings, that will strike most cruelly those like the veterans who seem to be temporarily benefitted. The first person injured by sky-rocket-ing prices is the man on a fixed income. Every disabled veteran on pension or allowance is on fixed income. This bill favors the able-bodied veteran at the expense of the disabled veteran.

"Wealth is not created, nor is it more equitably distrib-uted by this method. A Government, like an individual, must ultimately meet legitimate obligations out of the pro-duction of wealth by the labor of human beings applied to the resources of nature. Every country that has attempted the form of meeting its obligations which is here provided has suffered disastrous consequences.

"In the majority of cases printing-press money has not been retired through taxation. Because of increased costs, caused by inflated prices, new issue has followed new issue, ending in the ultimate wiping out of the currency of the afflicted country. In a few cases, like our own in the period of the Civil War, the printing of Treasury notes to cover an emergency has fortunately not resulted in actual disaster and collapse but has nevertheless caused this Nation untold troubles, economic and political, for a whole generation."

I am enclosing for your information a copy of a pamphlet entitled "Summary History of United States Money," and also a copy of an address entitled, "Gold and the Money of the United States," which Secretary Morganthau recently delivered before a conference here in Washington.

Sincerely yours,
(signed) HERBERT E. GASTON
Assistant Secretary of the Treasury.

Under date of June 18th, 1940, we forwarded a reply to the Assistant Secretary's letter on behalf of the President, in the following terms:

Mr. Herbert E. Gaston
Assitant Secretary of the Treasury
Treasury Department
Washington, D. C.
Dear Mr. Gaston:

Your good letter, with enclosures, in reply to my telegrams to our President, has been received and thoughtfully perused.

It is difficult for me to understand by what process of reasoning your Department arrives at the conclusion that it is necessary to borrow the Nation's money at interest in order to stabilize the value of the dollar, or to obviate wild inflation, as the excerpt from President Roosevelt's speech would indicate.

With a properly constituted Monetary Authority established in Washington, which would have the supervision of the issuance of and release of the Nation's money, it seems to me that the amount of money in circulation could be more effectively controlled than in the hands of private banking institutions.

As the matter now stands, checks are used as a medium of exchange, the value of check-book money being governed entirely by frequent unscrupulous bankers. This credit form of money, backed by the collateral of mortgagors, has been the cause of our major economic distresses. By the expansion and contraction of these credit instruments, at the will of the banking fraternity, the Nation has become pauperized.

Will you be so good as to explain to me why it is necessary to issue United States Bonds instead of United States Notes?

Most certainly multiplied millions of American citizens are asking the question why Congress does not use the powers vested in it by Article 1, Section 8, Part 5 of the Constitution to "coin money and regulate the value thereof." Until this edict is obeyed we can expect great discontent among the people and subversive elements to thrive.

Printing press money, controlled by a responsible Monetary Authority, should most certainly be preferable to check-book money over which there is no control.

It would be well if our Government, while making experiments, would experiment with the enforcement of the Constitution of the United States in regard to the money question. Our present Government, and your Department, possesses an opportunity to serve this Nation in an unprecedented manner, and to forestall the ambitions of a self-appointed world savior.

I prevail upon you, in the name of Humanity and of Democracy and of true Patriotism, to listen to the insistent appeals of true Americans, and issue debt and interest free money, thereby solving our Nation's dilemma. The enclosed mimeographed circular may be of interest to you.

Thanking you for your courtesy, and praying for a united, tranquil and prosperous Nation, I am

Yours sincerely

(signed) JOHN R. ELSOM

What Can We Electors Do?

Political Party has followed Political Party in power through the White House and Congress, decade after decade, with the result that the Nation continues to flounder in a morass of economic confusion, and it is quite obvious that if our money system is to be brought into conformity with the policies as enunciated by the Founders of the Nation, the demand must come from the electors of the Nation. Under our Democratic processes, anything which is in harmony with the Constitution of the United States which the majority of the people demand, can be obtained.

It is the duty, as well as the high privilege, of every voter to ascertain the position of candidates who would seek public office, relative to this paramount issue. *Only those who will declare themselves in favor of applying Article 1, Section 8, Part 5 of the Constitution to our Nation's monetary policy, and who go on record as espousing the cause of a money system based on wealth instead of on debt, should be sent to our legislatives halls as the Representative of the People.*

Upon their induction into office, all Federal Representatives are required to take an oath to "preserve, maintain and defend the Constitution of the United States"—of which Article 1, Section 8, Paragraph 5 is a part. Any Representative, failing to enforce or preserve the entire Constitution, has, therefore, violated the oath by which he is bound and is no longer deserving of the patronage or confidence of the people and should be prevented, by all lawful means, succeeding himself in the office which he has held, or attaining to any other public office which he may seek.

In addition to the voters' prerogative at the polls, whereby the will of the people is expressed, the voters of the Nation are privileged under our Democratic form of Government, to demand the obedience of Congress to the Constitution in its entirety.

WHAT THE VIOLATION OF
Article 1, Section 8, Part 5 of the Constitution
Of the United States of America
("CONGRESS shall have Power to Coin Money
and Regulate the Value Thereof")
HAS DONE TO US

1. It has allowed the usurpation by the Banking System of the power reposed in Congress to *issue* and *regulate* the value of money.

2. It has given us a system of legalized banditry unparalleled in the history of nations.

3. It has given us a Government—not of the People—but by a small group of Internationalists who dominate our Legislative Bodies.

4. It has made of *every citizen* a bondsman (slave) of the Money-Creating, Bond-Holding Bankers.

5. It has caused to be created a National debt of 50 billion dollars—all of which money should have been *issued* by Congress, instead of *borrowed.*

6. It has allowed Banks to obtain money from the U. S. Treasury for the cost of printing (27 cents per thousand dollars); to *create* money with a fountain pen by falsely entering a Bank Loan as a Bank Deposit.

7. It has made it possible for the Banks to loan at interest from 20 to 30 times the amount they have in cash. There is less than One Billion Dollars of currency in all Banks, while there are 70 Billion Dollars of Bank Deposits, so-called. 97% of Bank Deposits are Bank Loans—the borrowers supplying the credit. There is less than 1¾ cents in cash behind each dollar of bank deposits, throughout the Nation.

8. It has made it possible for the Banks to expand and then contract credit—by which process they have obtained control of 87% of our National wealth by owning outright through foreclosure, or holding mortgages on that percentage of assessed properties.

9. It has caused, apart from all other foreclosures, 600 families every day, for years, to be dispossessed. Every minute of every working hour a family is forced to vacate, to satisfy the demands of greed.

10. It has caused the domination of our School System by the money monopolists, in the matter of Economics, so that college graduates do not know that the Government does not issue our principal medium of exchange—that the

Federal Reserve is *not* a Government Bank—that the Government gave, without charge to the Federal Reserve Bank, 7/9ths of the Nation's hoard of Gold—that our present economy is unconstitutional—or that Wars are not fought for the preservation of Democracy, but rather for the preservation of the Money System, collection of European investments and to increase the National Debt.

11. It has established a monetary system by which *every dollar* must be borrowed into circulation and pay interest to the Shylock money-creating Bankers. 27 cents of every earned dollar goes for interest charges. Our annual interest bill is about $15,000,000,000. (This in 1940.)

12. It has resulted in the Federal Reserve System, a private banking institution, becoming the Fiscal Agent of our Government, in which capacity it absolutely controls the financial affairs of the Nation and all subdivisions thereof, as well as every person living therein.

13. It has produced a situation which has made seemingly necessary the planned destruction of, or curtailment of production, of consumable goods, while 69 million Americans are in dire need, many actually starving to death in the midst of abundance.

14. It has caused the prostitution of the Courts to the point that the poor man cannot obtain justice in civil actions where insurance companies, banks or their subservient stooges are involved.

15. It has caused foreign "isms" to make disastrous inroads upon America and Americanism, by causing discontent through granting unjust and unconstitutional special privilege to a chosen few.

WHAT THE ENFORCEMENT OF
Article 1, Section 8, Part 5 of the Constitution
Of the United States of America

("CONGRESS shall have Power to Coin Money
and Regulate the Value Thereof")
WILL DO FOR US

1. It will restore our Government, out of the hands of the International Bankers and Munitions Makers, *back to the people. Thus the principal motives for war will be removed.*

2. It will solve our National Debt Problem by the issuance of Debt and Interest Free *Constitutional Money* with which to pay for all future Governmental expenditures, thus effecting a saving to the taxpayers of from 120% to 150%. Outstanding Government Bonds, which have been paid for with money shall be retired with Constitutionally issued money—United States Notes. Bonds issued to the Banks without the payment of money shall be cancelled without remuneration to the Banks.

3. It will allow the U. S. Treasury to issue to the Federal Government, and all Governmental Subdivisions thereof, money at the rate which the Banks now obtain it—27 cents per $1,000—and to loan money to U. S. Citizens at not more than 2% interest.

4. It will reduce taxation from one-half to three-quarters —or probably end taxation entirely—by ending the payment of interest on unconstitutionally issued and unnecessary Government Bonds; by the collection of interest by the U. S. Treasury on money loaned; and by eliminating the necessity for our gigantic *Relief Program,* which requires 60% of all taxes to finance.

5. It will make it possible for our Government to pay pensions of at least $100 monthly to all retired Senior Citizens; Citizens who are unemployable through disability; Widows with minor children; and $50 monthly to children of pensioned persons, and orphans, who have reached the age of 18 years and who desire to pursue study in college

or university. Senior Citizens will be honored and will be a national asset instead of a liability. "Honor thy Father and thy Mother" is a command of God, upon which condition long national existence is assured.

6. It will supply purchasing power to the 69,000,000 persons who are now "ill-housed, ill-fed and ill-clad," in sufficient amount to qualify them as consumers of goods— thus they will provide a market for more goods than can be produced by our present national industrial establishments.

7. It will solve the unemployment problem immediately by breaking the log-jam between the producer and the consumer—the lack of money in the pockets of the majority. The *"No Men Wanted"* signs on factory gates will have the "No" crossed out.

8. It will make possible the establishment of a scientific, Economic and Monetary Authority by Congress, whose duty it will be to control the issuance of money through Governmental expenditures, to keep in perfect balance the productive capacity and consuming ability of the Nation.

9. It will forever end inflation and deflation of the circulating medium, by which the Banking System has engineered the exploitation of the People so that the real wealth of the Nation could be gathered to themselves. This Monetary Board—and not the unscrupulous Private Bankers— will not only issue the money, as the Constitution provides, but will also regulate its value. It never was—nor is it now —necessary to borrow money at interest to stabilize its value or obviate inflation. That medieval idea was invented by the goldsmiths and is propagated by our Money Masters.

10. It will end all un-American activities by rescuing the people of the Nation from the grip of the fountain pen money-creators, bond holders, interest collectors and mortgage foreclosers—the present wreckers of this Republic— and by making America a Nation of happy, prosperous people. Every citizen and every stranger within our gates will

be so completely sold on the "American Way" that no other way will be thought of.

11. It will solve our crime problem—which is caused largely by poverty through unemployment, and which costs the Nation over 15 Billion Dollars annually.

12. It will obviate the necessity of young womanhood selling their bodies to the highest bidder in order to sustain life. They will either find honorable employment or marriage when the young men are employed producing and distributing goods to 9,000,000 consumers who are not now consuming.

13. It will restore the Constitution to its place of Supreme Law in the Land, and the Nation will enjoy the benefits of Constitutional Government. The Declaration of Independence and the Preamble to the Constitution will cease to be but sublime phraseology. They will become potent actualities to every American.

14. It will dethrone Gold as the Nation's god and make money the *servant* instead of the *master* of the People. The Rule of Gold will be superseded by The Golden Rule, and true spiritual values will gain the ascendency over material values. Thus the Kingdom of God will be extended on the earth.

15. It will make of America the Christian Republic it was intended to be, with "Government of the People, by the People, *for the People,*" a fact instead *of a slogan.*

Patriotism in Action

Will Official Washington heed the message of the thunderbolt? Will the righteous and patriotic demands of logic and justice be met? Will the Republic be preserved by the obedience of its lawmakers to its Constitution—or will they, by continuing their subservience to the Money Powers, regardless of their oaths of office and the demands of the

People, wreck the Nation, laying the blame on the encroachment of foreign "isms," "Fifth Columnists," and "un-American Activities"?

The responsibility for the preservation of Democracy rests squarely on the shoulders of those who are now holding public office. It is in their hands to preserve or to destroy.

A terrible war raged in Europe over the *money issue.*

Statesmen *can* save the Nation; Politicians *will* destroy it. Hitler, in six years, had, by the issuance of debt and interest free money, rebuilt a Nation and perfected a War Machine which threatened the world. His ambition was to force that economy on the entire world.

We electors do not need a savior from across the sea. We can solve our own national problems and declare our own Economic Emancipation. The Constitution provides the sword of Democracy to wield in bloodless revolution.

This economic war, however, must be fought if a victory is to be won. This war for deliverance from the tyranny of the "Money Changers" must be won on Democracy's Battle Field—the polling booths of the Nation. The bombs used must be ballots in the hands of informed electors, not hand grenades in the hands of blood letting revolutionists. It must be won at the next general election, and it can be won there and then.

If each reader of this book will become a recruiting officer in the battle for Constitutional Money and will spread this gospel of equity and truth by securing copies of this book to place in the hands of influential persons, ministers, school teachers, parent-teacher associations, organization heads, labor union officials, newspaper editors, governors, assemblymen, senators and congressmen, sufficient numbers of our citizens will become such enthusiastic honest money advocates that only such congressional candidates as pledge themselves to work and vote for Constitutional Money will be sent to Washington at the next election.

Then, and then only will we have in America "Government of the people, by the people, for the people," the kind of a Nation which the Founding Fathers in the Declaration of Independence and the Constitution determined that it should be.

Monetary Reform is the major issue in American politics. Let us consider it as such, by making certain that only candidates who are dedicted to Monetary Reform will represent us in Washington.

CHAPTER X

BANK CREDIT RACKET

(From Australia)

"Of all the like particulars of the BANK CREDIT racket we have permitted the self-styled or so-called International Bankers to make of our money, that of their exchange charge on cheques drawn otherwise than on a bank near at hand, is perhaps the most paltry and grasping make-believe, of their GOLDEN CALF religion and worship.

"While financing multi-million pound so-called 'war-loans,' as they do their so-called 'fixed deposits' and 'savings accounts,' with fictional money; money that does not exist, ONLY as a bookkeeping record of what was ONCE money, but is now retired and is only a bookkeeping accommodation, is a MOST of their all-round monetary swindle—their exchange on cheques is a LEAST of their all-round monetary swindle.

"But, as such it is a key to a ruling factor of the legalized and customized bank swindles, namely PRETENCE. Pretence, that in order to pay their overhead costs they must collect a paltry 6d. 9d. 1/– exchange on cheques not drawn on a local bank. *This, incidentally, was unknown prior to August 1914.* Have you ever read of the trained pauper beggars of Paris? How an individual with his arms tucked away under his cloak, and his shoulders made to appear armless, would stand soliciting alms. As seen in their OWN light you have there a characteristic picture of the estimated 300 ruling international bankers, i.e., trained professional pauper beggars. *Paupers, in the sense that all the wealth they have, they have obtained by bank ledger fraud.*

"Or same thing ledger 'make-believe.' As they have it in their Protocol 1.23. 'Our countersign is—Force and Make-believe.' Prior to August 1914—and to have proper understanding of these things, it is essential to know what that date signifies—a bank pretence of 'having to be careful to make things pay,' was the THEN proverbial bad on cheques. And another purpose this particular CHEAT serves is to 'make work.' Work for work's sake, or mere 'busyness.' Like compulsory voting, another Banker originated racket to falsify the ballot, and keep an army of high school illiterates working for a small wage in Electoral Offices doing nothing rational or useful.

As we have it in their Protocol 4,3.

". . . This is the reason why it is indispensable for us to undermine all faith, to tear out of the minds of the GOYIM the very principle of Godhead and the spirit, and to put in its place *arithmetical calculations and material needs.*"

"We must always keep in mind that for the bank racket to function at all 'smoothly' it is absolutely essential that money is spent faster than it is issued, and that a great proportion of a country's population be kept busy on a small wage doing nothing but what is non-productive, destructive or stupid.

"You may say 'what do you mean by 'doing stupid'?' Well, of course there is more behind the fact than I have space for. But there is this. You will agree that it is stupid to 'try and take more out than you put in.' BUT, *that is just what all 'business' is trying to do all the time.* All business is ever trying to take more out (price) of the public purse, than all business ever puts in (wages) the public purse. And what does the bank do?

"They falsely enter the indispensable 'OVERDRAFT' in their ledgers as a deposit, the doing of which is nothing else than a legalized or rather customized issue of COUNTERFEIT MONEY. PLEASE GET THIS PLAIN. All business is run on 'overdraft' but all business deposits nothing. and has nothing equitable to deposit. The Bankers control the issue of legal tender (not the government) and they see to it that the issue of legal tender never equates the demand thereof.

"And their reason is very evident. It is the shortage of legal tender that creates a demand for their fictional bank 'credit.' Bankers have no respect for the dictionary meaning of words, they aspire to be their OWN dictionary as they would also be their own God. (It is this last aspiration that spells their ultimate fate) Credit and debit are to them interchangeable words, each to mean the other according to what most favours their talmudic 'theology' and their golden calf worship. Thus it is that made factual by their falsified ledgers, what they call 'credit' works out 'debit.' AND:—

"There is nothing left now for us but to ever get deeper and deeper into debt to the banking system . . . AN HONEST MONEY SYSTEM IS THE ONLY ALTERNATIVE. (See below)

"The bank 'OVERDRAFT' cheat, corresponds to the falsity they have influenced to be actually taught in the high schools and to appear in some dictionaries, namely that 'BANKS LEND THEIR DEPOSITS.' Whereas the factual truth is, that bankers make their OWN deposits, by overdrafts and loans. The only possible difference between a bank loan and a bank overdraft is the particular financial jargon they use.

Bank Deposit Money

"The most sinister and anti-social feature about *bank-deposit money is that it has no existence.* The banks owe the public for a total amount of money which does not exist. In buying and selling, implemented by cheque transactions, there is a mere change in the party to whom the money is owed by the banks. As the one depositor's account is debited, the other is credited and *the banks can go on owing for it all the time.*

"*The whole profit of the issuance of money has provided* the capital of the great banking business as it exists today. *Starting with nothing* whatever of their own, they have got the whole world into their debt irredeemably, *by a trick.*

"This money comes into existence every time the banks 'lend' and disappears every time the debt is repaid to them. So that if industry tries to repay, *the money of the nation disappears.* This is what makes prosperity so 'dangerous' as it destroys money just when it is most needed and precipitates a slump.

"There is nothing left now for us but to ever get deeper and deeper into debt to the banking system in order to provide the increasing amounts of money the nation requires for its expansion and growth. AN HONEST MONEY SYSTEM IS THE ONLY ALTERNATIVE."

The above is a statement made by Frederick Soddy, M.A., F.R.S., Nobel Prize Winner, 1921, and was taken from a certain money classic, the particulars of which are available.—D. W. de Louth, "Wykeham Cottage," Innisplain, via Beaudesert, Queensland, Australia.

APPENDIX—1961

The Federal Reserve Banking System was set up in 1913. It is a privately owned stock corporation owned by "Member Banks." In 1922 these bankers got a law passed allowing the profits of their operations (which originally were to go to the government) to be kept by them as "reserves."

Since 1913, with the three world wars and government spending, and "foreign aid," more than a trillion dollars worth of bonds have been issued. These bonds have gone to the banks for credits on their books (that is free, for the bookkeeping). The people must pay the inerest on the bonds through taxes. Since bonds are rarely paid off the people will be paying taxes for the interest forever.

All this has come about with the help of our statesmen and "liberal" political parties.

CPSIA information can be obtained
at www.ICGtesting.com
Printed in the USA
BVHW081047110222
628627BV00002B/126